P9-DHG-354

dessert for two

CONTENTS

Introduction

Howdy! I'm pleased to make your acquaintance. I truly am. Let me brush the coffee cake crumbs off the kitchen table so you and I can "have a set" and get to know each other. First and foremost, I'm a Texan. Second, my name is Christina.

I was born and raised just outside Dallas and I come from a long line of hardworking farmers. My maternal grandparents were cotton farmers in north Texas, and my dad's family grew tobacco in the Carolinas. Southern food and farming runs through my veins like white whiskey.

In 2006, I left Texas to live in California. The first house I lived in was a tiny one-bedroom house with a yard bigger than the house and a basement that flooded each winter. I worked all day at my dream job (in agriculture, of course), and then came home and worked all night on my Master's thesis. It was quite the load. To help me get through epic writing sessions at night, I ate dessert. I craved every kind of dessert I'd ever known growing up. On Monday night, I craved a devil's food cake made tender with the addition of mayonnaise. On Tuesday night, it was my mom's Ranger Cookies made with crunchy cornflakes. Wednesday morning, you could find me calling my mom at work, begging for another one of my grandmother's recipes.

However, I had no one to help me eat these desserts. If I made four dozen cookies, I would surely eat all four dozen. I had an idea to take regular recipes and scale them down to make fewer servings. My first attempts at reducing Texas Chocolate Sheet Cake to two small ramekins were disastrous: eggy and sunken in the middle. Baking is a science, and you just can't switch around ingredients and pan sizes willy-nilly. But little by little, I made progress: plain chocolate chip cookies were mastered (the perfect butter-to-flour ratio took months). That basic cookie recipe is the foundation for all other cookie recipes. I mastered four vanilla cupcakes and made many variations. One day, I came across a 6-inch cake pan at the hobby store, and rushed home to use it. It was then that I knew *Dessert for Two* was not just a passion; it was going to be a big part of my life.

I hope these recipes for small batches of desserts satisfy your cravings just right. I hope married couples put this book to use and grow closer ⅓ cup of chocolate chips at a time. I hope this book is a welcome addition to empty nesters: a way to still have dessert without the leftovers. And most of all, to everyone who lives alone: You should have your own personal-size cake and eat it, too.

Christina Lane
February, 2015

Equipment You Will Need

To make dessert for two, you may find you need some special equipment. Please don't feel as though you have to go out and buy every shape and size pan I use. Try to use what you have and if an alternative size other than the one I have listed works for you, great!

You've heard it before, but it bears repeating: Baking is a science. Measuring ingredients precisely is essential for success. This is even more pivotal in small-batch baking. One-eighth of a teaspoon might seem like nothing, but it is imperative to be precise.

Measuring

Kitchen scale
I have given many of my recipe ingredients in spoons/cups and weights. Baking by weight is more precise, plus it uses less dishes. Invest in a good kitchen scale with the ability to tare out the weight of your bowl. You'll use it more than you think.

Measuring cups
I'm sure you have some of these lying around.

Measuring spoons
You will need a set of measuring spoons that goes down to 1/8 teaspoon. If it also has 3/4 teaspoon, even better. These will be getting a lot of work in your kitchen.

Glass measuring cup
This is what you measure liquids in. Not for dry ingredients.

Bakeware

6-inch pie pan
A 6- to 7-inch pie pan works great for my mini pie recipes. Typically, a 6-inch pie pan will measure 6 inches in diameter on the bottom but will flare out to 7 inches on top. I prefer an oven-safe glass pie pan so I can monitor the browning of the crust. The glass one in this book is my grandmother's, and I love it dearly.

6-inch round cake pan
Essential for mini cakes. This pan is easy to find at craft or hobby stores, because it's technically the top layer of a wedding cake. (In our case, it's the only layer.)

4 ½-inch round mini springform pan
Makes the most adorable mini cheesecakes.

6-inch cast-iron skillet
Did you know they made miniature cast-iron skillets? They're adorable!

Bread loaf pan
A standard bread loaf pan that measures 9×5×3 inches is what we'll use to perfectly portion bars and even some pies.

Ramekins
I'm a bit of a ramekin fanatic. I collect them in every size, shape, and color. For the purposes of this book, you only need two sizes: the standard 6-ounce cup (the common size for crème brûlée) and the 10-ounce cup.

Mini gratin dishes
I use smaller versions of gratin dishes to make cobblers, bread pudding, and crisps. My favorite is an 8-inch oval that holds 4 cups of water to the brim. Typically, the things we bake in these dishes are forgiving, as long as you keep an eye on them in the oven, so use whatever size small dishes you can find.

Muffin pans
We may not fill every divot in the muffin pan, but we will make a small batch of cupcakes, mini cakes, and cookies! I rely on a standard muffin pan for such recipes as my Mini Sour Cream Pound Cakes, and a mini muffin pan for my Chocolate Pecan Tassies, Divinity, and Frozen Margarita Tarts.

Ice-cream maker
An ice-cream maker is a bit of a luxury item (and quite the cabinet space hog), but when you taste homemade ice cream made with only a few ingredients, I think you'll agree it's worth it. Look for them to go on sale at the end of summer.

Petite Utensils

Small utensils are not required for baking desserts for two, but I have a feeling the moment you try to wield a mini piece of pie from a mini pie dish with a regular-size pie server, you'll wish you had smaller tools. Here are a few of my favorite tiny utensils.

Mini whisk
A mini whisk fits well in your hand, and will whip a small amount of cream in no time.

Mini wooden spoons
In my opinion, you can never have enough wooden spoons in the kitchen. I use a small one for stirring homemade puddings and custards.

Small spatulas
I'm a firm believer in silicone spatulas. They help you get every last drop of batter from the bowl into the pan—very important when baking in small quantities. I use the mini ones intended for jam jars, but they're great for baking.

Small pie server
You'll need this for mini pies. Enough said.

Pastry brush
I brush all of my piecrusts with beaten egg yolk. It helps the crust turn golden brown, and it'll make your pies look as if they came from a bakery.

Mini Microplane
There was a time when I thought Microplanes were extravagant. Now, I panic when I'm cooking in a kitchen without one. I use it for freshly grated nutmeg, citrus zest, and hard cheeses.

Other Tools

Electric mixer
A large stand mixer is overkill for dessert for two — the paddle would spin without touching the small amount of batter. For this reason, I use a handheld electric mixer exclusively. I've used the same one for years, and it's never let me down.

Mixing bowls
If you buy a set of mixing bowls, you will only need the small and medium-size bowls for dessert for two. (Use the large bowl for salad to balance all the desserts you'll be eating.)

Colander/strainer
A small colander will help you rinse berries and sift flour or powdered sugar.

Culinary torch
Oh, the things we will torch, you and I! I bought my torch for crème brûlée originally, but I find myself using it to crisp up bread pudding, leftover piecrust, and more.

Silicone baking mats
I use these instead of greasing my cookie sheet. I love that they're reusable, and nothing, I mean *nothing*, will stick to these.

Parchment paper
I rely on parchment paper in cases where I can't use a silicone baking mat. While the brown paper gives my desserts the rustic vibe that I love, it really is a workhouse. Nothing sticks to parchment paper, not even tape (I tried it for photography purposes!). If you don't want to use parchment paper, grease your pans very well. When it comes to cakes, grease and flour the pans.

Candy thermometer
I love the way a good candy thermometer attaches the side of my pan so I have both hands free to stir. However, I don't love that most of them are not calibrated. If you buy one, calibrate it yourself in boiling water (212°F) before using. Depending on the size of your pan, the thermometer bulb may or may not touch the boiling sugar in the case of Divinity or Pralines. Adjust the thermometer, or test it by hand every so often.

The Baking Gospel *(and other notes)*

If someone asks for your recipe, share it. It's better to be known as the person who shares recipes than the person everyone must beg to make that cake one more time.

Cupcakes made with oil are always more tender than those made with butter (unless sour cream is involved). Save the butter for the frosting—and pile it on!

While we're talking about cupcakes . . . I always bake a small batch of cupcakes in the cups along the edge of the pan. I noticed they rise higher than the cups in the middle.

Creaming ingredients together is important. Blending the sugar into the fat in a recipe is a chance to dissolve the sugar, aerate the fat, and otherwise distribute flavors. Don't skimp. Let it be fluffy!

I'm always going to ask you to line your loaf pan with parchment paper, for easier removal of the baked loaf. The truth is, it can be tricky to wield a spatula in such a small pan. If you line with enough parchment to overhang, it serves as handles to lift out the dessert after baking.

Sweetened condensed milk. Let's face it: This stuff is sent from heaven. But desserts for two often only require a few tablespoons instead of the entire can. What to do? Buy the sweetened condensed milk sold in a squeeze bottle. I can always find it in the international aisle of even the smallest grocery stores. If you are able to find only the canned version, flip to the "Leftovers?" chapter to find other recipes that will use up the remaining portion.

A final note about ingredients: I recommend buying high-quality ingredients with which to bake. This is especially true for such things as cocoa powder and chocolate. For my recipe testing, I used name-brand ingredients. I'm not willing to take a risk with a dessert not turning out because of a store-brand product that contains water or cheap ingredients as filler. Use whatever you are comfortable with, but if your sour cream has the consistency of yogurt instead of thick cream, well, that's not right. The higher the fat content of your cocoa powder, the happier you'll be in life. Tested and proven.

COOKIES

1 Dozen or Less!

First, let's master baking a perfect batch of cookies together. They're ready in minutes, and great straight out of the oven. Cookies offer the fastest reward for your efforts: ten minutes of mixing and ten minutes of baking. Happiness is twenty minutes away from where you stand right now.

It all began with my classic chocolate chip cookie recipe. The search for the perfect chocolate chip cookie has led me through many, many recipes. Almost all of the recipes had an all-butter base. Although this tastes great, I wanted my chocolate chip cookies to have the look, fluff, and chewiness of a real bakery cookie. For this reason, I use a bit of shortening in my cookies. Don't worry, shortening won't hurt ya. My grandparents lived to be almost ninety and ate it daily.

1 DOZEN BAKERY-STYLE CHOCOLATE CHIP COOKIES

Yield • 12 cookies

4 tablespoons (60 grams) unsalted butter, at room temperature

2 tablespoons (24 grams) solid vegetable shortening

¼ cup (45 grams) light brown sugar

3 tablespoons (37.5 grams) granulated sugar

1 large egg yolk

¾ teaspoon vanilla extract

½ cup + 2 tablespoons (75 grams) all-purpose flour

⅛ teaspoon fine salt

⅛ teaspoon instant espresso powder

¼ teaspoon baking soda

¼ teaspoon baking powder

⅓ cup semisweet chocolate chips

PREHEAT THE OVEN TO 375°F and line a cookie sheet with parchment paper or a silicone mat.

In a medium-size bowl, using an electric mixer on medium speed, cream the butter, shortening, brown sugar, and granulated sugar together. Beat very well, about 45 seconds. Add the egg yolk and vanilla and beat until combined.

In a small bowl, whisk together all the remaining ingredients, except the chocolate chips, and add this mixture in two batches to the butter mixture, beating until just combined. Stir in the chocolate chips.

Scoop twelve equal-size dough balls and space them evenly apart on the prepared cookie sheet.

Bake the cookies for 8 to 9 minutes. Move them to a cooling rack immediately; serve warm.

CREAMSICLE MELTAWAYS

If you've never had a meltaway cookie, think of it as a cross between candy and cookie. It's like a cookie with the texture of soft butter mints. I love to keep ropes of this cookie dough in my freezer in all different flavors. I vary the type of citrus zest I use, or I leave it out all together for a vanilla version. Around the holidays, I substitute peppermint extract for vanilla and then dip the meltaways in melted chocolate. Meltaways are typically small, roundish cookies, but I think the minute I started cutting them the way I cut gnocchi is when they elevated to addictive status. The little flared edges are my favorite.

Yield • 12 cookies

4 tablespoons (60 grams) unsalted butter, at room temperature

3 tablespoons (19.5 grams) powdered sugar, plus ⅓ cup (35 grams) for rolling

Zest of ½ orange

2 teaspoons fresh orange juice

1 teaspoon vanilla extract

½ cup (60 grams) all-purpose flour

2 teaspoons cornstarch

Pinch of salt

IN A MEDIUM-SIZE BOWL, using an electric mixer on medium speed, beat together the butter and 3 tablespoons of the powdered sugar until creamy, about 1 minute. Add the orange zest, orange juice, and vanilla. Beat until combined.

Sprinkle the flour, cornstarch, and salt on top. Beat until combined.

Place the dough on a piece of waxed or parchment paper, and roll into a 12-inch rope with a 1-inch diameter. Refrigerate for at least 30 minutes.

Preheat the oven to 350°F, and line a cookie sheet with parchment paper.

Remove the dough from the fridge, and slice it into twelve 1-inch slices. Pinch the dough slightly in the middle as you move it to the prepared cookie sheet.

Bake the cookies for 13 to 14 minutes, until fragrant and the tops of the cookies are dry. The cookies should not brown.

Let cool on the cookie sheet for 1 minute, and then roll each cookie in the remaining ⅓ cup of powdered sugar before serving.

TEXAS RANGER COOKIES

When I visit home, these cookies are always in the cookie jar waiting for me. There's something so addictive about soft, chewy cookies punctuated with crispy cornflakes. The best way to describe these cookies is that they taste like caramel, with crunchy bits.

Yield • 8 cookies

¼ cup (48 grams) solid vegetable shortening

3 tablespoons (19.5 grams) granulated sugar

¼ cup (45 grams) packed light brown sugar

1 large egg white

¼ teaspoon vanilla extract

¼ teaspoon salt

½ cup (60 grams) all-purpose flour

¼ teaspoon baking powder

3 tablespoons (18 grams) natural (unsweetened) dessicated coconut

2 tablespoons (11 grams) rolled oats

⅓ cup (heaping) (12 grams) cornflakes

PREHEAT THE OVEN TO 350°F, and position a rack in the center of the oven.

Line a cookie sheet with a silicone mat or parchment paper. Additionally, if your cookie sheet is very thin or a dark color, double up two cookie sheets to help with heat distribution. I've found that thin cookie sheets allow cookies to spread too much during baking. Silicone mats are effective at heat distribution, and I highly recommend them.

In a medium-size bowl, using an electric mixer on medium speed, cream together the shortening, granulated sugar, and brown sugar very well, about 45 seconds. Add the egg white, vanilla, and salt. Beat for 15 seconds to combine well.

Sprinkle the flour and baking powder evenly over the dough. Add all the remaining ingredients on top. Beat the dough together for about 10 seconds to combine and crush the cornflakes.

Scoop eight equal-size dough balls and space them evenly on the prepared cookie sheet. Bake for 12 minutes.

Let cool for 1 minute on the cookie sheet, and then move to a cooling rack to cool completely.

>>· SNICKERDOODLES

There are some days when nothing but a crinkly cinnamon sugar cookie will do. This recipe uses cream cheese in the dough, for a bit of tang. You just may eat all ten cookies by yourself!

Yield • 10 cookies

3 tablespoons (45 grams) unsalted butter, at room temperature

2 ounces cream cheese, softened

½ cup + 2 tablespoons (125 grams) granulated sugar, divided

1 large egg

¾ cup + 2 tablespoons (105 grams) all-purpose flour

1 teaspoon cream of tartar

½ teaspoon baking soda

⅛ teaspoon salt

2 teaspoons ground cinnamon

PREHEAT THE OVEN TO 350°F, and position a rack in the center of the oven. Line a cookie sheet with a silicone mat or parchment paper.

In a medium-size bowl, using an electric mixer on medium speed, beat the butter, cream cheese, and ½ cup (100 grams) of the sugar. Beat until well mixed and fluffy, about 1 minute. Next, beat in the egg.

In a small bowl, stir together the flour, cream of tartar, baking soda, and salt. Sprinkle this mixture over the butter mixture and beat until just combined.

In a shallow bowl, stir together the remaining 2 tablespoons of sugar and the cinnamon. Scoop a heaping tablespoon of the dough, roll it in your palm lightly, and then roll it in the cinnamon-sugar mixture to coat. Repeat with remaining dough. You should get ten cookies.

Space the dough balls evenly apart on the prepared baking sheet, then bake for 10 to 12 minutes.

Let cool on the baking sheet for 1 minute, and then move to a cooling rack to cool completely.

LEMON MERINGUE PIE COOKIES

I am a lemon dessert lover. These cookies taste like a bite of lemon meringue pie, and I can't get enough of them. Make the meringue cookie shells, and fill them with whatever filling you like: chocolate pudding, vanilla pudding, or this lemon cream filling.

Yield • 4 cookies

FOR THE MERINGUE

1 large egg white

⅛ teaspoon cream of tartar

¼ cup (50 grams) granulated sugar

TO MAKE THE MERINGUE: First, preheat the oven to 200°F. Line a small sheet pan with parchment paper or a silicone mat.

In a medium-size bowl, using an electric mixer on medium speed, beat the egg white and cream of tartar until soft peaks form. Then, slowly stream in the sugar while beating. Beat until the mixture has stiff peaks.

Using two spoons or a piping bag, make four equal-size disks about 4 inches in diameter of the meringue mixture on the prepared sheet pan.

Bake for 40 minutes, and then turn off the oven and let the meringues cool inside the oven for 1 hour. Do not open the oven door.

FOR THE LEMON CURD

2 tablespoons (30 grams) unsalted butter, at room temperature

¼ cup (50 grams) granulated sugar

1 large egg + 2 large egg yolks

⅓ cup (80 mL) fresh lemon juice

Pinch of salt

¼ cup (60 mL) heavy whipping cream

1 tablespoon (6.5 grams) powdered sugar

FOR ASSEMBLY

1 graham cracker, crushed

TO MAKE THE LEMON CURD: In a medium-size bowl, using an electric mixer on high speed, beat together the butter and sugar until well combined. Add the egg and egg yolks one at a time while beating constantly. Finally, stream in the lemon juice and salt. The mixture may look a bit curdled – it's fine.

Pour the lemon curd into a small saucepan and bring to a simmer over medium-low heat to thicken. Stir constantly to avoid burning. Once simmering, remove from the heat and let cool.

In a separate medium-size bowl, using an electric mixer on high speed, whip the cream with the powdered sugar until soft peaks form. Set aside.

TO ASSEMBLE: Dollop the lemon curd on top of each meringue, add a spoonful of whipped cream, and sprinkle graham cracker crumbs on top before serving.

»· FORGOTTEN COOKIES

With this recipe comes zero guarantees that you will be able to resist a breakfast of cookies. The premise of these cookies is this: Preheat the oven at night, mix up the cookie dough, place it in the oven, turn off the oven, and sleep for 8 hours. In the morning, you'll have crisp meringue cookies. They sound much better than a bowl of bran flakes, don't they?

Yield • 6 cookies

1 large egg white, at room temperature

⅓ cup (65 grams) granulated sugar

½ teaspoon vanilla extract

½ cup (95 grams) chocolate chips

½ cup (75 grams) chopped nuts (pecans, almonds, anything you like)

½ cup (50 grams) sweetened shredded coconut

PREHEAT THE OVEN TO 350°F. Ensure it reaches this temperature before proceeding.

Line a cookie sheet with foil. Do not skip the foil.

In a medium-size bowl, beat the egg white until very stiff either by hand, using a large whisk, or using an electric mixer on high speed. Soft peaks will make cookies that spread – make sure you beat the egg white until stiff.

Beat in the sugar and vanilla. Fold in the remaining ingredients.

Scoop six equal-size portions of the batter onto the prepared cookie sheet, leaving at least 2 inches of space between the cookies.

Place the cookies in the oven, close the door, and then turn *off* the oven. Let the cookies sit without opening the door for 8 full hours. No peeking!

Store the cookies in an airtight jar so they stay crisp.

CHOCOLATE SUGAR COOKIES
with Raspberry Curd

These chocolate sugar cookies are everything a sugar cookie should be: soft, chewy, sparkling with sugar, and perfect for smashing raspberry curd between. If you don't have time to make the raspberry curd, it's fine—the cookies stand on their own just as well. These cookies are messy to eat with the raspberry curd, but oh so good!

Yield • 4 sandwich cookies

FOR THE COOKIES

4 tablespoons (60 grams) unsalted butter, at room temperature

¼ cup + 2 tablespoons (68 grams) light brown sugar

1 large egg yolk

¼ teaspoon vanilla extract

3 tablespoons (21 grams) unsweetened cocoa powder

½ cup (60 grams) all-purpose flour

¼ teaspoon baking soda

¼ teaspoon salt

2 tablespoons (25 grams) granulated sugar, for rolling

TO MAKE THE COOKIES: In a medium-size bowl, using an electric mixer on medium speed, beat the butter until fluffy, about 1 minute. Add the brown sugar and beat for another minute. Next, add the egg yolk and vanilla and beat until well combined.

In a separate bowl, whisk together the cocoa powder, flour, baking soda, and salt until no lumps remain. Add the dry ingredients to the wet ingredients in two increments, mixing between each addition. Cover the dough and chill it for at least 1 hour. The dough can be made in advance or even frozen.

When ready to bake, preheat the oven to 350°F. Line a cookie sheet with parchment paper. (You can use cooking spray, alternatively).

Place the granulated sugar in a shallow bowl.

Scoop eight equal-size portions of dough, roll them in your hand to form perfect balls, and then roll through the sugar to coat. Space evenly apart on the prepared cookie sheet.

Bake for 8 to 10 minutes, until set in the center and beginning to crackle.

Let cool completely on the cookie sheet.

FOR THE RASPBERRY CURD

- 4 tablespoons (60 grams) unsalted butter
- 6 ounces raspberries (frozen is fine)
- Juice from 1 small lemon
- ¼ cup + 2 tablespoons (75 grams) granulated sugar
- ⅛ teaspoon salt
- 3 large egg yolks
- ¼ teaspoon vanilla extract

TO MAKE THE RASPBERRY CURD: In a medium-size saucepan, melt the butter over medium heat. Add the raspberries, lemon juice, sugar, and salt. Bring to a simmer over medium-high heat, stirring occasionally. There should be tiny bubbles along the edges of the pan.

Place the egg yolks in a small bowl on the side. Add a small scoop of the simmering raspberry mixture to the egg yolks and stir vigorously. Repeat a few times. Then, pour the entire egg yolk mixture back into the saucepan, and bring to a brisk simmer over medium-high heat, stirring occasionally. Cook for 1 minute, then remove from the heat and stir in the vanilla. Pour the raspberry mixture into a bowl, press plastic wrap directly on the surface, and refrigerate for at least 4 hours.

To serve, scoop the raspberry curd onto four of the cookies. Top with the remaining four cookies to make messy, delicious sandwiches.

»· SALTED CARAMEL MACARONS

I'm going to be a bit bossy with this recipe, so please forgive me in advance. French macarons are persnickety little cookies, and there are a few rules you must follow when making them. First things first: Old egg whites are the only ones that will work. Fresh egg whites will prevent little feet (the lacy part on the bottom) from forming. I typically save one egg from the carton, separate the white into a glass, and let it further age in the fridge for one week. When the egg white is done aging, it will be loose and almost liquefied, instead of its usual thick texture. Yes, this egg is probably at least one week past its expiration date. Don't worry.

Next, almond meal. You can buy almond meal preground from almonds that have already been blanched (skinless). This is fine. But I typically get better results when I use plain almond meal that has been ground with the skins, and sift it to remove the skins. When you sift the almond meal, you will have about 1 tablespoon of almond skins to discard. No big deal. The recipe will still work because this recipe is by weight. Furthermore, you could even grind your own almonds and then sift. I specifically created this recipe to work with any type of almond meal, because almond meal can be pricey and hard to find. Grinding your own almonds gives the best results, although there will be tiny specks of almond skin in your cookies (even after sifting). Think of it as cookie freckles.

The cookies are prone to burning if they are baked on a large sheet pan, or on a dark metal pan. Try to use a small quarter-sheet pan that is light in color. Do not use a nonstick pan. You must bake the cookies on parchment paper. Furthermore, the parchment paper must fit the pan exactly, or the excess parchment paper buckled around the edges will cause the cookies to spread unevenly.

Finally, you must make this recipe by weight, not measuring. I've tested this recipe in both a gas oven and an electric oven with great results. For what it's worth, a propane oven makes the cookies rise the highest.

Yield • 12 cookies

FOR THE MACARONS

1 large egg white (aged; see headnote)

⅓ cup (34 grams) almond meal

⅓ + ¼ cup (76.5 grams) powdered sugar

1 tablespoon dried meringue powder

3 drops almond extract

FOR THE SALTED CARAMEL SAUCE

⅓ cup (65 grams) granulated sugar

2 tablespoons (30 grams) unsalted butter

3 tablespoons (45 mL) heavy whipping cream

¼ teaspoon kosher salt

TO MAKE THE MACARONS: Let the egg white come to room temperature for at least a few hours on the counter.

Line a small quarter-sheet pan with parchment paper. It's best if the pan is light colored and not nonstick. Cut the parchment paper to fit perfectly in the pan, otherwise the excess paper will buckle and cause the cookies to spread unevenly.

Sift the almond meal. Discard any almond skins, if necessary. Weigh the almond meal and ensure that you have 1.2 ounces (34 grams). Next, sift the powdered sugar on top. Whisk to combine the two.

In a medium-size bowl, using an electric mixer on medium speed, beat the egg white until foamy, about 10 seconds. Then, begin to slowly add the meringue powder while beating continuously. Beat until soft peaks form.

Add one-third of the almond meal mixture to the egg whites. Using a rubber spatula, fold it in gently. Proper folding technique is down the middle with the thinnest edges of the spatula, and then sweeping the outside edges of the bowl. Take your time. Repeat with the remaining almond meal mixture in two increments. Finally, fold in the almond extract.

Move the batter to a piping bag fitted with a metal tip (or a plastic bag with a metal piping tip placed in a bottom corner; snip off the plastic to make it fit).

Pipe out twelve 1-inch circles. The best way to make a perfect circle is to hold the tip vertically and let the batter naturally fall out in a puddle around it.

Let the batter rest on the baking sheet until it's dry to the touch. It's ready when you lightly touch the surface of the cookie and the batter doesn't stick to your skin. It's almost as if a little skin has formed on the cookies. This could take anywhere from 30 to 60 minutes. On a humid day, it's closer to 60 minutes.

Preheat the oven to 300°F. If you think your oven runs hot, preheat to 295°F. Bake the cookies for 14 to 16 minutes. Let cool on the baking sheet, and then move them to a cooling rack.

TO MAKE THE SAUCE: Place the granulated sugar in a 1-quart saucepan over medium-high heat, stirring constantly. Continue to stir while the sugar melts completely. It will clump in the beginning, but all the clumps will melt and it will start to turn a light golden brown. Once it is entirely melted, add the butter and stir until the butter melts. Then, stir in the cream. Be careful — the caramel will rise up a bit in the pan. Let the mixture boil for 1 minute, stirring continuously.

Remove the caramel from the heat, and stir in the salt. Pour into a container and refrigerate to help it cool. It should be firm, but still pliable.

Place six dollops of the cooled caramel sauce on the underside of six macarons. Top with the remaining macarons to make cookie sandwiches. You can serve immediately, but they are even better if allowed to soften for at least an hour.

Congratulations! You just baked the most difficult cookie in the world. That French flair looks good on you, too.

I grew up around coconut macaroons. They were a popular cookie in our house because my mom often had all the ingredients in the pantry to make them. I ate them, I liked them. But it wasn't until I had a coconut macaroon at Upper Crust Bakery in Chico, California, that it really stopped me in my tracks. I was in Chico, celebrating sweet friends' nuptials, and the wedding party met at Upper Crust for breakfast the morning after the wedding. I had just ordered one of its famous quiches, and was about to take a sip from my latte when a chocolate-covered macaroon crossed my line of sight. The macaroon was enormous. My friends ordered one for the table. I had one bite of my quiche, and then moved in for the kill. I ate the rest of the macaroon by myself. Sorry, friends. You know how I am around dessert.

I don't have Upper Crust's recipe, nor could my friend who used to work there confirm that the bakery uses unsweetened coconut. But I have a hunch that it does, because this macaroon wasn't cloying like the ones I grew up on. The fruity note in the cookie I had is something I can only pin to honey, so I used honey as the sweetener. The pinch of salt is really what sends these over the edge.

»·COCONUT MACAROOOOONS

Yield • 6 cookies

Cooking spray

1 cup packed (3 ounces) unsweetened finely shredded coconut

¼ teaspoon kosher salt

3 tablespoons (45 mL) clover honey

1 large egg white

¼ teaspoon almond extract

PREHEAT THE OVEN TO 350°F, and spray a small sheet pan with cooking spray.

In a bowl, stir together the coconut and salt. Add the honey, egg white, and almond extract, and stir very well.

Scoop six mounds of dough and pack it together tightly as you drop it on the prepared baking sheet. Bake the cookies for 17 to 18 minutes, until golden brown.

Let cool completely on the cookie sheet, then move with a spatula to a serving plate.

»· OATMEAL CREAM PIES

The thing is, these oatmeal cookies are so good on their own — so chewy, spicy, and warm — that they don't even really need the marshmallow filling. But they're certainly not worse with marshmallow filling, so pile it on!

Yield • 5 sandwich cookies

FOR THE COOKIES

½ (45 grams) cup rolled oats

¾ cup (90 grams) all-purpose flour

¾ teaspoon cornstarch

½ teaspoon baking powder

⅛ teaspoon baking soda

⅛ teaspoon salt

½ teaspoon ground cinnamon

⅛ teaspoon freshly grated nutmeg

⅛ teaspoon ground ginger

3 tablespoons (45 grams) unsalted butter, at room temperature

2 tablespoons (24 grams) solid vegetable shortening

3 tablespoons (45 mL) molasses

½ cup (100 grams) granulated sugar

½ teaspoon vanilla extract

1 large egg yolk

FOR THE MARSHMALLOW FILLING

1 cup (2.5 ounces) marshmallow cream

2 tablespoons (30 grams) unsalted butter, at room temperature

2 tablespoons (24 grams) solid vegetable shortening

½ cup (50 grams) powdered sugar

PREHEAT THE OVEN TO 350°F and line a cookie sheet with parchment paper.

TO MAKE THE COOKIES: In a food processor, give the oats ten 1-second pulses to break them up a bit. Do not grind them to a powder, just break them up.

In a small bowl, whisk together the oats, flour, cornstarch, baking powder, baking soda, salt, and spices. Whisk very well.

In a medium-size bowl, using an electric mixer on medium speed, cream together the butter, shortening, molasses, sugar, and vanilla for at least 45 seconds, scraping the bowl as necessary to incorporate evenly. Finally, beat in the egg yolk. Add the dry ingredients to this mixture in two batches, beating well to combine.

Make ten golf ball–size dough balls with your hands. Space them equally apart on the prepared cookie sheet and then press them flat with your hands.

Bake for 10 to 12 minutes, or until fragrant and the tops look dry. Don't overbake, because they will continue to cook a bit while they cool on the pan.

Let cool on the cookie sheet for 5 minutes, then move to a cooling rack.

TO MAKE THE FILLING: Once the cookies have cooled, using an electric mixer on high speed, beat together all the filling ingredients in a medium-size bowl. Divide it among five of the cookies, and then press another cookie on top of each to form five sandwiches.

CHOCOLATE PECAN TASSIES

Tassie cups are one of my favorite Southern Christmas cookies. They taste like miniature bites of pecan pie. The cream cheese dough is rich, and you must make individual tart cups in a mini muffin pan, but in my book, it's still less effort than an entire pecan pie. For a fun substitution, try whiskey instead of vanilla extract.

Yield • 8 cookies

4 + 1 tablespoons (75 grams) unsalted butter, at room temperature, divided

2 ounces cream cheese, softened

½ cup (60 grams) all-purpose flour

Cooking spray

⅓ cup (60 grams) light brown sugar

¼ teaspoon vanilla extract

⅓ cup (50 grams) chopped pecans

1 tablespoon mini chocolate chips

1 large egg, beaten

FIRST, MAKE THE DOUGH: In a medium-size bowl, using an electric mixer on medium speed, beat together 4 tablespoons of the butter and the cream cheese. Once thoroughly combined, add the flour and beat until a dough forms. Cover the bowl and let rest in the fridge for at least 20 minutes. This can be done up to 2 days ahead of time.

Preheat the oven to 350°F, and grease eight cups of a mini muffin pan with cooking spray.

In a small microwave-safe bowl, melt the remaining tablespoon of butter in the microwave on high power for about 30 seconds. Remove from the microwave and add the brown sugar, vanilla, pecans, chocolate chips, and egg to the bowl. Whisk to combine.

Remove the dough from the fridge, and divide it into four equal portions. Halve each portion and roll into balls (you should have eight balls of dough total). Drop each dough ball into a prepared muffin cup.

Press the dough down with your thumb, and then use your fingers to stretch the dough all the way to the edges of its muffin cup. Make sure the dough cups are of an even thickness all the way around.

Divide the filling equally among the dough cups. Bake for 20 minutes.

Let cool in the pan for a few minutes, and then move the tassie cups to a cooling rack to cool completely.

BROWNIE COOKIES

You know these cookies. They are big, crispy, crunchy, and chewy all at once. They are positively cravable in a way that no other cookie is. Lucky for you, I scaled them down so you can have damage control taken care of before you even start eating!

Yield • 10 cookies

2 large egg whites

¼ teaspoon vanilla extract

1 cup (100 grams) powdered sugar

⅓ cup (37 grams) unsweetened cocoa powder

⅛ teaspoon salt

3 tablespoons chocolate chips

PREHEAT THE OVEN TO 350°F and line a baking sheet with a silicone mat or parchment paper.

In a medium-size bowl, using an electric mixer on high speed, beat the egg whites and vanilla until soft peaks form.

In a separate bowl, whisk together the powdered sugar, cocoa powder, and salt. Ensure the mixture is free of lumps.

Add half of the dry ingredients to the egg white mixture and fold until no streaks remain. Fold in the remaining dry ingredients, and finally stir in the chocolate chips.

Scoop ten equal-size portions of batter onto the prepared baking sheet.

Bake the cookies for 15 to 17 minutes. The surface of the cookies will appear dry and they will start to crack around the edges.

Let cool on the baking sheet for a few minutes before moving to a cooling rack.

»· BUTTERED GRITS COOKIES
with Lime Glaze

Normally, I'm a spicy grits kind of girl. I love a hot bowl of grits sprinkled with sharp Cheddar cheese and pickled jalapeños. In the summertime, I love a bowl with fresh cherry tomatoes from the garden. So, grits in a dessert? Why not? These cookies have the texture of a muffin top — soft and cakey. You can frequently find me eating these for breakfast, and I won't stop you from doing the same!

Yield • 12 cookies

3 tablespoons (40 grams) stone-ground grits (I use white hominy grits)

½ cup + 1 tablespoon (135 mL) water

¼ teaspoon salt

Cooking spray

4 tablespoons (60 grams) unsalted butter, plus butter for pan (optional)

½ cup (100 grams) granulated sugar

1 large egg

½ teaspoon vanilla extract

1 cup (120 grams) all-purpose flour

½ teaspoon baking powder

1 cup (100 grams) powdered sugar

Juice of 1 lime

PLACE THE GRITS, WATER, AND SALT in a 2-cup glass measuring cup and stir. Microwave on HIGH for 90 seconds. Stir the mixture, and then microwave for another 30 seconds. The mixture should not overflow the cup, but if it does, start over, as the amount of liquid in the recipe will then be off.

Pour the grits into a medium-size mixing bowl, and let cool for 15 minutes.

Preheat the oven to 350°F, and spray a cookie sheet with cooking spray or rub it with butter.

Once the grits have cooled, stir in the butter. It will melt completely. Next, stir in the sugar, egg, and vanilla. Stir until very well combined.

Sprinkle the flour and baking powder on top of the grits mixture. Stir to combine.

Scoop out twelve equal portions of the dough onto the cookie sheet about 1 ½ inches apart.

Bake for 11 to 13 minutes, or until the surface of the cookies appears dry and the edges are just beginning to brown.

Meanwhile, in a small bowl, mix together the powdered sugar and lime juice. Drizzle over the cookies. Serve warm.

»· FOUR-INGREDIENT PEANUT BUTTER COOKIES

I call these emergency cookies. I can whip these up with almost zero planning or preparation. Depending on what I have in the pantry, they become chocolate peanut butter cookies, with the addition of chocolate chunks. Or, a few marshmallows are pressed in the tops of the cookies. But seriously, they are just as good plain.

Yield • 6 cookies

½ cup (135 grams) creamy peanut butter

5 tablespoons (62.5 grams) granulated sugar

1 large egg

Handful of mini marshmallows (optional)

Handful of chopped semisweet chocolate (optional)

PREHEAT THE OVEN TO 350°F.

Place the peanut butter, sugar, and egg in a medium-size bowl. Stir until well combined. Drop by heaping tablespoons spaced 2 inches apart onto an ungreased baking sheet.

Press mini marshmallows or chocolate chunks into the surface of the cookies, if desired.

Bake for 10 to 11 minutes, or until the edges are slightly browned. Let cool on the baking sheet for 3 minutes before moving to a cooling rack to cool completely.

»· BUTTER COOKIES . . .
with Sprinkles!

This basic butter cookie recipe can see you through many holidays: birthdays with sprinkles (obviously), festive colored sprinkles for the holidays, or no sprinkles at all when you just want a plain, rich little butter cookie. The recipe makes six fat cookies, but you could slice them thinner for slightly crisper cookies. Whatever you do — don't take them out of the oven before the brown edges have developed. The golden brown edges are the best part!

Yield • 6 cookies

4 tablespoons (60 grams) unsalted butter, at room temperature

¼ cup (50 grams) granulated sugar

1 large egg yolk

½ teaspoon vanilla extract

½ cup (60 grams) all-purpose flour

Pinch of salt

2 tablespoons (28 grams) sprinkles

IN A SMALL BOWL, using an electric mixer on medium speed, beat together the butter and sugar until fluffy, about 1 minute. Add the egg yolk and vanilla and beat until combined.

Sprinkle the flour and salt on top and beat until just combined. Stir in the sprinkles.

Shape the dough into a log about 4 inches long. Wrap in plastic wrap or parchment paper and refrigerate for at least 1 hour, or freeze for 30 minutes.

Preheat the oven to 375°F. Line a small cookie sheet with parchment paper. Slice the cookies into six equal slices, and space evenly on the baking sheet. Bake for 10 minutes. The cookies are done when the bottom edges begin to brown. Let cool on the baking sheet for 5 minutes before moving to a cooling rack to cool completely.

1 DOZEN CUT-OUT SUGAR COOKIES

I love how all grocery stores in the country strategically place clear containers of frosted sugar cookies with sprinkles near the checkout aisle. I can't resist them. I love a good cut-out sugar cookie topped with frosting and sprinkles. I think you'd be hard-pressed to find anyone who doesn't. This is your new go-to small-batch sugar cookie recipe. This recipe is for rolling and cutting out shapes; the sugar cookie sandwiches on page 22 are drop-style cookies. No matter what your sugar craving, I've got you covered. Make these at the holidays with your favorite cookie cutters.

Oh, and you don't have to use Texas-shaped cookie cutters for this recipe, but your cookies won't be nearly as cute without it.

Yield • 12 cookies

FOR THE COOKIES:

- **¾ cup all-purpose flour, plus extra for rolling**
- **½ teaspoon baking powder**
- **Pinch of salt**
- **4 tablespoons (60 grams) unsalted butter, at room temperature**
- **¼ cup sugar**
- **1 large egg yolk**
- **½ teaspoon vanilla extract**
- **⅛ teaspoon almond extract**

TO MAKE THE COOKIES: Preheat the oven to 350°F and line a baking sheet with parchment paper or a silicone mat.

In a small bowl, whisk together the flour, baking powder and salt. In a medium bowl, beat together with an electric mixer the butter and sugar. Once light and fluffy, beat in the egg yolk and extracts. Once they are well incorporated, sprinkle half of the flour mixture over the butter mixture and beat gently until combined, then sprinkle with the rest of the flour mixture. Beat until no streaks of flour remain, but be careful not to overmix.

Dust a clean countertop with flour, and dump the dough out onto it. Gather it into a ball and press it into a 2-inch-thick disk. Flour your rolling pin, then roll out the dough big enough to cut out about eight shapes with your choice of cookie cutter(s). Place the shapes on a baking sheet lined with parchment paper or a silicone mat. Gather the dough scraps and reroll to cut out four more shapes and place them on the cookie sheet.

Place the cookie sheet in the freezer for 5 minutes.

Bake the cookies for 10 to 12 minutes, until their edges just start to turn brown. Let them sit on the sheet a few minutes before moving them a wire rack to cool completely.

FOR THE ICING:

1 1/2 cups powdered sugar

2 to 3 tablespoons milk

1/8 teaspoon vanilla extract

Sprinkles, for decorating

TO MAKE THE ICING: Once the cookies are completely cool, whisk together all the icing ingredients. Start with 1 tablespoon of milk, and add up to 2 more tablespoons to achieve a slightly runny consistency. Ice your cookies by outlining the shape using a squeeze bottle or small piping bag with a tip, then flood the icing within the borders to fill it in. Top with sprinkles and enjoy!

BARS

Brownies, Blondies, Crispy Rice Things, and More!

>>· BROWNIES FOR TWO

If there's a dessert for two that's made most frequently in my kitchen, it's brownies. Instead of using a large, flat pan for brownies, I bake them in a loaf pan. When sliced down the middle, you have two bakery-sized brownie squares. Who wouldn't want to share with you?

Yield • 2 brownies

4 tablespoons (60 grams) unsalted butter, diced

½ cup + 1 tablespoon (112.5 grams) granulated sugar

¼ cup + 2 tablespoons (42 grams) unsweetened cocoa powder

¼ teaspoon salt

½ teaspoon vanilla extract

1 large egg

¼ cup (30 grams) all-purpose flour

PREHEAT THE OVEN TO 325°F, and position a rack in the lower third of the oven. Line a 9 × 5 × 3-inch loaf pan with parchment paper.

In a medium-size microwave-safe bowl, combine the butter, sugar, and cocoa powder. Microwave on HIGH for 30 seconds. Stir, and microwave for another 30 seconds.

Stir the mixture very well, then add the salt and vanilla. Stir for 1 minute to let the mixture cool down. Add the egg, and stir until it's incorporated.

Sprinkle in the flour, and then give the batter about fifty brisk strokes, using a wooden spoon. Normally, we wouldn't mix batter this long for fear of overworking the flour, but the sugar makes up for it in this recipe. This helps achieve the cracked topping and chewiness.

Spread the batter evenly in the prepared loaf pan. Bake for 23 minutes. A toothpick inserted into the center should have moist crumbs. The surface of the brownies is shiny and dry when done, and will crack as it cools.

Let cool completely in the pan, then use the parchment paper to remove the brownies from the pan. Slice in half and serve.

I love lemon bars as much as I love my husband. No, really, I do. One would not exist without the other. I believe taste buds are heritable, and I inherited my love of lemon desserts from my grandmother. I'd been happily enjoying lemon bars my whole life before I met my husband. I love them thick with almost an inch of shortbread crust to bite through, and I love them thin with the tangiest of lemon fillings. I thought I had enjoyed lemon bars every way possible.

And then, Brian asked me to marry him. Fast-forward six months and we're taste-testing different caterers for the wedding. One caterer served a brûléed lemon bar as a dessert option for the rehearsal dinner. My life changed. Were things meant to be with Brian so that I could taste the most perfect dessert? I think so.

BRÛLÉED LEMON BARS

Yield • 2 bars

8 tablespoons (120 grams) cold unsalted butter, diced

⅓ cup (35 grams) powdered sugar

1 cup + 1 tablespoon (127.5 grams) all-purpose flour, divided

½ cup + 2 tablespoons (125 grams) granulated sugar, divided

1 teaspoon fresh lemon zest

3 tablespoons (45 mL) fresh lemon juice

2 large eggs

¼ teaspoon baking powder

PREHEAT THE OVEN TO 350°F, and line a glass 9 × 5 × 3-inch loaf pan with parchment paper, leaving enough parchment overhang to form handles. If using a metal loaf pan, be sure to cover the entire surface so the metal doesn't react with the lemon during baking.

Place the butter in a medium-size bowl. Add the powdered sugar and 1 cup of the flour. Work the butter into the sugar and flour, using your fingertips or a pastry cutter. When the mixture comes together into crumbs that hold together when squeezed in your palm, you're done.

Pack this mixture firmly into the prepared loaf pan. Bake for 25 minutes.

While the crust bakes, in a large bowl, using an electric mixer on medium speed, beat together ½ cup of the granulated sugar and the lemon zest, lemon juice, and eggs for 1 minute, until foamy. Add the baking powder and remaining 1 tablespoon of flour and continue to beat until no lumps of flour remain.

Pour the lemon filling over the parbaked crust. Bake for another 20 to 23 minutes. The filling should set entirely and not have any jiggle to it.

Let the lemon bars cool entirely in the pan, and then lift them out, using the parchment paper as handles.

Refrigerate for at least 4 hours before serving, for best flavor. Before serving, sprinkle the remaining 2 tablespoons of granulated sugar on top, and caramelize with a culinary torch. Slice in half, and then serve immediately (the sugar crust will soften as it sits).

»· MUD HENS

Desserts with the strangest names always taste the best, in my book. Mud hens are a type of cookie bar. The bottom layer is cookie dough studded with chocolate chips. The cookie layer is then topped with nuts and marshmallows, and everything is crowned in a beautiful crisp meringue. You want to let these bars cool in the pan for at least an hour, but remove them after that so the crust can firm up.

Yield • 2 bars

1 tablespoon (12 grams) solid vegetable shortening, plus more for pan

4 tablespoons (60 grams) unsalted butter, at room temperature

6 tablespoons (75 grams) granulated sugar

1 large egg, separated

½ cup + 1 tablespoon (67.5 grams) all-purpose flour

⅛ teaspoon baking powder

⅛ teaspoon salt

2 tablespoons (30 grams) semisweet chocolate chips

¼ cup (26 grams) chopped pecans

¼ cup (10 grams) mini marshmallows

2 tablespoons (23 grams) light brown sugar

PREHEAT THE OVEN TO 350°F, and grease a 9 × 5 × 3-inch loaf pan with shortening.

In a medium-size bowl, using an electric mixer on medium speed, beat together the remaining 1 tablespoon of shortening, butter, and granulated sugar. Beat this mixture very well before adding the egg yolk and continuing to beat.

Sprinkle the flour, baking powder, and salt over the top and beat until the dough comes together in a mass. At first it will be crumbly, but keep beating and it will firm up. Spread the dough evenly in the bottom of the prepared loaf pan, using a silicone spatula.

Sprinkle the chocolate chips on top, lightly pressing them into the dough. Then sprinkle the marshmallows and pecans.

Using an electric mixer on high speed, beat the egg white until stiff. Add the brown sugar and fold it in well. Spread it on top of the nuts and marshmallows. Don't worry if the marshmallows and nuts get all mixed up into the meringue — this is good.

Bake for 22 to 24 minutes, until the meringue is nicely browned. Let cool in the pan for an hour before removing them from the pan (or else the bottom might get soggy). Slice in half and serve.

MISSISSIPPI MUD BARS

It's not often that I share these bars. In fact, I purposefully make them when no one is around. My own personal heaven is locked away somewhere between the fudgy brownie layer, the gooey marshmallow layer, and thick frosting. See whether you can share them.

Yield • 2 bars

FOR THE BARS

4 tablespoons (60 grams) unsalted butter

½ cup + 1 tablespoon (112.5 grams) granulated sugar

¼ cup + 2 tablespoons (42 grams) unsweetened cocoa powder

¼ teaspoon salt

½ teaspoon vanilla extract

1 large egg

¼ cup (30 grams) all-purpose flour

¼ cup (48 grams) chocolate chips

1 cup (56 grams) mini marshmallows

FOR THE FROSTING

3 tablespoons (45 grams) unsalted butter, melted

2 tablespoons (14 grams) unsweetened cocoa powder

½ cup (50 grams) powdered sugar

1 tablespoon (15 mL) milk

¼ teaspoon vanilla extract

TO MAKE THE BARS: Preheat the oven to 325°F, and line a 9×5×3-inch loaf pan with parchment paper.

In a medium-size, microwave-safe bowl, combine the butter, sugar, and cocoa powder. Microwave on HIGH for 30 seconds. Stir the mixture very well, and then microwave for another 30 seconds. Carefully remove the bowl from the microwave.

Add the salt and vanilla to the warm butter mixture, and stir for about a minute to cool down the batter. Next, stir in the egg until well combined.

Sprinkle in the flour, and then give the batter about fifty brisk strokes, using a wooden spoon. Stir in the chocolate chips, and then spread the mixture in the prepared loaf pan.

Bake for 23 minutes. A toothpick inserted into the center should have moist crumbs.

Top evenly with the mini marshmallows, and return the pan to the oven for 2 to 5 minutes. The marshmallows will puff up, but it's best to remove the pan from the oven before they start to brown.

TO MAKE THE FROSTING: Remove the pan from the oven, and then begin making the frosting. Beat together all the ingredients until thick and spreadable. Pour evenly over the marshmallow layer while still warm, and refrigerate until set.

ROCKY ROAD BROWNIE BITES

This riff on my perfect brownies for two makes mini bites topped with crunch rocky road pieces. For my dad, who thinks a brownie isn't a brownie without nuts in it.

Yield • 4 bites

FOR THE BROWNIES

3 tablespoons (45 grams) unsalted butter, plus extra for greasing pan

7 tablespoons (87.5 grams) granulated sugar

¼ cup (28 grams) unsweetened cocoa powder

¼ teaspoon salt

½ teaspoon vanilla extract

1 large egg

3 tablespoons (22.5 grams) all-purpose flour

TO MAKE THE BROWNIES: Preheat the oven to 350°F and grease four cups along the edge of a muffin pan with the extra butter.

In a medium-size, microwave-safe bowl, combine the butter, sugar, and cocoa powder. Microwave on HIGH for 30 seconds. Remove the bowl from the microwave, and stir the ingredients together. It's okay if the butter isn't all the way melted when it comes out of the microwave, but once you stir it together, it should melt entirely. Add the salt and vanilla and continue to stir for about 1 minute to cool down the mixture. Add the egg and stir very well.

Sprinkle in the flour, and then give the batter about fifty brisk strokes, using a wooden spoon, aerating and scraping the sides of the bowl as you go.

Divide the batter equally among the prepared muffin cups. Bake for about 15 minutes. Let cool for a few minutes before removing them from the pan to a cooling rack to cool completely. Note that the brownies may sink slightly in the middle if you under baked them to keep them gooey.

FOR THE ROCKY ROAD TOPPING

- **2 ounces (56 grams) bittersweet chocolate chips**
- **1 tablespoon (15 grams) unsalted butter**
- **1 tablespoon (15 mL) honey or light corn syrup**
- **Pinch of salt**
- **¼ cup (39 grams) roasted unsalted peanuts**
- **¼ cup (14 grams) mini marshmallows**

TO MAKE THE TOPPING: Have ready a sheet pan lined with waxed paper or a silicone mat.

Combine all the ingredients, except the peanuts and marshmallows, in the top of a double boiler and melt over low heat (you can also pulse in a microwave-safe bowl at 50% power until melted). Once the chocolate is shiny, stir in the peanuts. Finally, stir in the marshmallows. Pour the mixture on the prepared sheet pan and let cool until it can be broken into pieces. You can put it in the refrigerator to speed things along.

Once the rocky road bark has set, break it into large pieces, and press it gently into the tops of each brownie bite.

BLONDIES FOR TWO

These blondies are every bit as good as brownies — it just depends on whether you want your fix with chocolate or with butterscotch goodness. These bars are thick, dense, and packed with butterscotch chips and pecans. I have a hard time deciding between these and a brownie all the time!

Yield • 2 blondies

3 tablespoons (45 grams) unsalted butter, melted

½ cup (90 grams) light brown sugar

1 large egg yolk

½ teaspoon vanilla extract

⅛ teaspoon salt

½ cup (60 grams) all-purpose flour

¼ teaspoon baking powder

¼ cup (50 grams) butterscotch chips

¼ cup (26 grams) toasted chopped pecans

PREHEAT THE OVEN TO 350°F. Line a 9 × 5 × 3-inch loaf pan with parchment paper, leaving enough parchment overhang to form handles.

In a medium-size bowl, stir together the melted butter and brown sugar with a wooden spoon until well blended. Stir in the egg yolk, vanilla, and salt.

Sprinkle the flour and baking powder evenly on top, and stir until combined.

Finally, stir in the butterscotch chips and pecans.

Spread the batter evenly into the prepared loaf pan. Bake for 18 to 20 minutes. A toothpick inserted into the center should have moist crumbs. Immediately lift the blondies out of the pan and allow to cool completely on a cooling rack before devouring.

This is the part where I become stereotypical: the men in my family are way into NASCAR. My dad, brother, and nephew pack up a giant picnic to take to the race track on race day. My mom makes these flavored crispy rice treats, and I have a suspicion they are gone before they've even left the parking lot. I scaled down my mom's recipe, which most likely came from a copy of Southern Living years ago. I've never been happier to have portion control than with these bars!

WHITE CHOCOLATE PEANUT CRISPY RICE TREATS

Yield • 2 treats

3 tablespoons (45 grams) unsalted butter, plus more for pan

1 ½ cups (85 grams) mini marshmallows

½ cup (85 grams) white chocolate chips

¼ cup (39 grams) chopped roasted peanuts

⅓ cup (56 grams) toffee chips

1 ½ cups (1 ¾ ounces) crispy rice cereal

BUTTER A 9 × 5 × 3-INCH LOAF PAN. In a medium-size saucepan, combine the butter and marshmallows over medium heat and stir frequently. Once the marshmallows have melted, lower the heat, and add the white chocolate chips. Stir for a few seconds to melt the chips. They should melt quickly. Add all the remaining ingredients and stir very well to combine.

Press the mixture into the prepared loaf pan and let set for about 15 minutes before slicing and serving.

»· WHITE CHOCOLATE ALMOND CARAMELITAS

The first time I made caramelitas, I ate the entire pan in shock. I had no idea something could taste so delicious. Carmelitas are dense and rich, like a blondie, but have the added perk of caramel.

Yield • 2 bars

½ cup (60 grams) all-purpose flour

5 tablespoons (28.5 grams) rolled oats

¼ cup (45 grams) light brown sugar

Pinch of salt

7 tablespoons (105 grams) unsalted butter, at room temperature

¼ cup (20 grams) sliced almonds

½ cup (85 grams) white chocolate chips

½ cup (120 mL) store-bought caramel sauce (or double my recipe for Salted Caramel Sauce, page 26)

PREHEAT THE OVEN TO 350°F and line a 9×5×3-inch loaf pan with foil, leaving enough foil overhang to form handles.

Combine the flour, oats, brown sugar, and salt in a small bowl. Add the butter, and work it through the dough, using a pastry blender or two knives.

Divide the dough in half. Press half of the dough into the bottom of the prepared loaf pan. Bake for 10 minutes.

Meanwhile, in a small bowl, stir together the almonds and white chocolate chips. Evenly distribute the mixture over the top of the parbaked crust. Drizzle with the caramel sauce. Pinch off pieces of the remaining dough and scatter it over the top. Bake for 20 minutes, until the caramel is bubbling and the crust is starting to brown.

Let cool completely before removing from the pan. Slice in half and serve.

HELLO DOLLY BARS

I'm a sucker for these chunky bars. They come together in a flash—no need to make a dough or real crust. Just crumble some graham crackers, stir with butter and sugar and push into the pan. And instead of dirtying another bowl, just sprinkle the pecans, chocolate, and coconut right on top. My favorite part is squeezing the condensed milk on top of everything, and sliding the pan back into the oven. Well, that's my second favorite part. My favorite part is actually eating them!

Yield • 2 bars

4 graham cracker sheets, crushed (½ cup crumbs)

2 tablespoons (30 grams) unsalted butter, melted (plus more for greasing pan)

1 tablespoon (12.5 grams) granulated sugar

⅓ cup (50 grams) chopped pecans

¼ cup (42 grams) chopped semisweet chocolate

¼ cup (25 grams) packed sweetened shredded coconut

½ cup (120 mL) sweetened condensed milk

PREHEAT THE OVEN TO 350°F, and lightly grease a 9×5×3-inch loaf pan.

Stir together the graham cracker crumbs, melted butter, and sugar.

Press the mixture into the prepared pan, using a small measuring cup to compact the crumbs neatly.

Bake for 8 minutes.

Remove the pan from the oven, and then sprinkle the pecans, chocolate, and coconut on top of the parbaked crust. Finally, pour the condensed milk over all. Bake for 18 minutes, or until bubbly and golden brown. Let cool in the pan before slicing in half and serving.

CHESS PIE BARS

If you've never had chess pie, it tastes like a giant sugar cookie custard pie. The filling is super sweet and rich, but for some reason, you just keep going back for one more bite. Before you know it, the whole pan is gone. Don't say I didn't warn you!

Yield • 2 pie bars

FOR THE CRUST

1 cup (120 grams) all-purpose flour

2 teaspoons granulated sugar

¼ teaspoon salt

4 tablespoons (60 grams) cold unsalted butter, diced

½ teaspoon cider vinegar

3 to 5 tablespoons (45 to 75 mL) water

FOR THE FILLING

1 cup (200 grams) granulated sugar

1 tablespoon (10 grams) yellow cornmeal

1 ½ teaspoon all-purpose flour

⅛ teaspoon salt

4 tablespoons (60 grams) unsalted butter, melted

2 tablespoons (30 mL) milk

1 ½ teaspoons cider vinegar

½ teaspoon vanilla extract

2 large eggs, beaten

TO MAKE THE CRUST: Preheat the oven to 400°F.

Combine the flour, sugar, and salt in a medium-size bowl. Add the butter, and work it through the flour using a pastry blender or two knives until evenly incorporated. Add the vinegar and 3 tablespoons of water, and stir with a fork until a shaggy dough forms. If the dough doesn't clump together nicely and there are dry bits of flour at the bottom of the bowl, add up to 2 more tablespoons of water.

Press the crust into the bottom of a an ungreased 9 × 5 × 3-inch loaf pan. Bake for 10 minutes and remove the pan from the oven. Then, turn down the oven temperature to 350°F.

TO MAKE THE FILLING: Stir together all the filling ingredients. Pour over the parbaked crust. Bake for 40 minutes. The pie bars are done when the top is nicely browned and dry.

Let cool completely in the pan, and chill overnight for the prettiest slices. I think the pie tastes best cold, but you can serve it warm, if you like.

OVENCE
Nº18

PEANUT BUTTER SWIRL BROWNIES

If brownies can get better, it's with a sweet peanut butter swirl. You can use any type of nut or seed butter here. I love tahini as well.

Yield • 2 brownies

4 tablespoons (60 grams) unsalted butter, diced

½ cup + 1 tablespoon (112.5 grams) granulated sugar

¼ cup + 2 tablespoons (42 grams) unsweetened cocoa powder

¼ teaspoon salt

½ teaspoon vanilla extract

1 large egg

¼ cup (30 grams) all-purpose flour

2 tablespoons (30 mL) creamy peanut butter

1 tablespoon (6.5 grams) powdered sugar

PREHEAT THE OVEN TO 325°F and position a rack in the lower third of the oven. Line a 9 × 5 × 3-inch loaf pan with parchment paper.

In a medium-size microwave-safe bowl, combine the butter, granulated sugar, and cocoa powder. Microwave on HIGH for 30 seconds. Stir, and microwave for another 30 seconds.

Stir the mixture very well, then add the salt and vanilla. Stir for 1 minute to cool down the mixture. 4. Add the egg, and stir until it's incorporated.

Sprinkle in the flour, and then give the batter fifty brisk strokes, using a wooden spoon. Spread the batter evenly in the prepared loaf pan.

In a small, microwave-safe bowl, heat the peanut butter in the microwave on HIGH until spreadable, about 15 seconds. Stir in the powdered sugar. Swirl this mixture into the brownies.

Bake for 23 minutes. A toothpick inserted into the center should have moist crumbs. The surface of the brownies is shiny and dry when done, and will crack as it cools.

Let cool completely in the pan, then use the parchment paper to remove the brownies from the pan. Slice and serve.

APPLE BROWN BETTY
with Gingersnap Crumbs

Brown Betty is usually made with plain bread crumbs, and while it is delicious, I thought we could do a little better than that. I used crushed gingersnap cookies instead. It eliminates the need for adding any spices, making this recipe that much quicker to throw together any day of the week. In the oven, the crumbs reconstitute in the apple juices and take on a cake-like texture. I know you'll enjoy this dessert.

Yield • 2 servings

3 tablespoons (45 grams) unsalted butter, thinly sliced, plus more for pan

2 medium-size apples (12 to 13 ounces total)

5 ounces gingersnap cookies (the hard, crunchy kind)

2 tablespoons (25 grams) granulated sugar

¼ cup (60 mL) fresh orange juice

Vanilla ice cream, for serving

PREHEAT THE OVEN TO 350°F and grease a mini baking dish with the extra butter. The size of the baking dish doesn't matter too much here – you could use ramekins, too. The baking dish should hold 3 to 4 cups of liquid.

Peel, core, and thinly slice the apples. Set aside.

Crush the gingersnap cookies. You should end up with 1 cup of crumbs.

Sprinkle ⅓ cup of the gingersnap crumbs in the bottom of the prepared dish. Top with half of the apple slices. Sprinkle 1 tablespoon of the sugar on top. Repeat: another ⅓ cup of crumbs, the remaining apples, and the last tablespoon of sugar. Pour the orange juice evenly on top.

Top the mixture with the remaining ⅓ cup of gingersnap crumbs and the sliced butter.

Bake for 40 minutes, until bubbling around the edges and nicely browned on top. Serve warm with ice cream.

»· PEACH PIE BARS

It's my belief that peaches ripen on the tree explicitly for the chance to be tucked in a shortbread crust. These peach pie bars with shortbread crust are perfection. The crust has all the sweetness needed; the peaches marinate in a mere tablespoon of brown sugar. Oh, and whiskey. They also marinate in that, too. Ahhh, heaven.

Yield • 2 bars

12 ounces frozen sliced peaches (thawed and drained), or 3 small fresh, chopped (about 5.5 ounces each before chopping)

2 teaspoons whiskey

1 teaspoon fresh lemon juice

1 tablespoon (11.5 grams) light brown sugar

½ teaspoon ground cinnamon (optional)

7 tablespoons (105 grams) unsalted butter, at room temperature

⅓ cup (65 grams) granulated sugar

⅔ cup (80 grams) all-purpose flour

1 tablespoon (7 grams) cornstarch

PREHEAT THE OVEN TO 350°F, and line just the bottom of a loaf pan with parchment paper. To do this, trace the bottom of the loaf pan shape onto a piece of parchment paper. Cut it out, flip it over, and nestle it in the pan.

Combine the peaches, whiskey, lemon juice, brown sugar, and cinnamon, if using, in a bowl. Set aside.

Combine the butter, granulated sugar, and flour in a small bowl. Knead in the butter, using two knives or your fingertips. The consistency should be like that of sugar cookie dough. Reserve ¼ cup of this mixture and press the remaining dough evenly into the bottom of the prepared loaf pan.

Add the cornstarch to the peaches, and stir to combine. Arrange the peaches (juices included) on top of the pressed dough. Crumble the reserved ¼ cup of dough on top.

Bake for 40 minutes. Let chill overnight for best cutting results. Run a knife around the edge of the pan, then use a spatula to get under the parchment paper and lift the bars out. Slice and serve.

FOR THE LIME CURD FILLING

2 large egg yolks

7 ounces (210 mL) sweetened condensed milk

Zest of 1 lime

⅓ cup (80 mL) bottled Key lime juice

FOR THE CHOCOLATE TOPPING

12 ounces (340 grams) semisweet chocolate chips

2 tablespoons (30 mL) neutral oil, such as canola

TO MAKE THE LIME CURD FILLING: In a medium-size bowl, using an electric mixer on medium speed, beat the egg yolks and condensed milk until light and airy, about 3 minutes. The mixture will be pale in color, and slightly foamy. Next, add the lime zest and Key lime juice and beat until combined. Pour into the piecrust, and freeze overnight.

Before serving, dip a sharp knife in hot water, and slice the pie into four mini pieces. Insert a stick in each crust end, and place back in the freezer.

TO MAKE THE TOPPING: Melt the chocolate and oil in the top of a double boiler over medium heat. Do not let the water boil, and stir the chocolate constantly. Remove it (carefully!) from the stove just before all of the chips melt. Stir to melt everything.

To dip each pie piece, hold it by the stick end, and place the pie upside down in the chocolate (in other words, dip the creamy part first). Flip it quickly, and use a spoon to cover the crust in chocolate. You don't have to cover the entire slice in chocolate—a little crust peeking out is good. Place the pie pops back in the freezer for a few minute to firm up, and then serve!

»· PEAR PANDOWDY

Yield • 2 servings

FOR THE PEAR FILLING

2 pounds (900 grams) fresh pears (I used 4 red Anjous)

¼ cup (45 grams) light brown sugar

Juice of ½ lemon

½ teaspoon ground cinnamon

¼ teaspoon freshly grated nutmeg

⅛ teaspoon ground ginger

⅛ teaspoon ground coriander

1 tablespoon (7 grams) cornstarch

FOR THE CRUST

½ cup (60 grams) all-purpose flour

1 teaspoon granulated sugar

⅛ teaspoon salt

2 tablespoons (30 grams) cold unsalted butter, diced

¼ teaspoon white vinegar

2 to 3 (30 to 45 mL) tablespoons cold water

TO SERVE

Whipped cream or ice cream (optional)

TO MAKE THE FILLING: Preheat the oven to 375°F, and have ready a 9 × 5 × 3-inch loaf pan.

Peel and core the pears. Use a melon baller or a tiny teaspoon to scoop out the core. Quarter each pear, and then slice each quarter into five or six slices. In a large bowl, toss the pears with the brown sugar, lemon juice, spices, and cornstarch. Set aside while you make the crust.

TO MAKE THE CRUST: In a medium-size bowl, combine the flour, sugar, and salt. Mix well. Add the butter to the flour mixture. Incorporate the butter into the flour by pinching it with your fingertips, or by using a pastry cutter. Once the butter is very well incorporated and smaller than peas, add the vinegar and 2 tablespoons of the cold water. Stir with a fork until a shaggy dough forms. If it seems too dry or has dry flour pockets at the bottom of the bowl, add up to 1 tablespoon of water. Most often, it doesn't need it.

Flour a counter and roll out the dough to be slightly larger than the base of the loaf pan.

Pour the pear mixture in the loaf pan and top it with the crust, neatly tucking under the edges. Bake for 30 minutes.

After 30 minutes, score the crust with two X's, and press it down into the pear juice. Bake for another 10 minutes, pressing down the crust again two more times.

TO SERVE: Serve with whipped cream or ice cream.

You and I are going to call this dessert a pandowdy. When you serve it to your guest, refer to it as a fancy pear tarte Tatin in your best French accent. After enjoying apple tarte Tatin one day at a French restaurant, I realized its similarity to a pandowdy. A pandowdy is baked fruit with a crust on top that is pushed into the fruit juices during the baking process. A tarte Tatin is baked fruit with a crust on top that is then flipped and served. See? No difference.

LEMON GINGERSNAP ICE CREAM

I'm tempted to call this dessert for one. Lemon and ginger are some of my favorite flavors to find in desserts. If you've never made a s'more with a ginger snap instead of a graham cracker, please, try that immediately! If you're a lemon lover like me, you'll love a little smear of lemon curd in there, too. This ice cream has all of those flavors mashed together. I freeze it in a loaf pan, which equates to almost a pint of ice cream, perfect for two (I guess).

Yield • 1 pint

FOR THE VANILLA ICE CREAM

2 large egg yolks

⅓ cup + 1 tablespoon (77.5 grams) granulated sugar

¾ teaspoon vanilla extract

1 cup (240 mL) whole milk

1 cup (240 mL) heavy whipping cream

FOR THE LEMON CURD

2 tablespoons (30 grams) unsalted butter, at room temperature

¼ cup (50 grams) granulated sugar

1 large egg + 2 large egg yolks

⅓ cup (80 mL) fresh lemon juice

Pinch of salt

TO SERVE

Store-bought gingersnaps, crushed

TO MAKE THE ICE CREAM: First, ensure the bowl of your ice-cream maker is frozen solid.

In a medium-size bowl, whisk together the egg yolks, sugar, and vanilla. Whisk very well – at first, it will seem as if it won't come together, but it will. Whisk until pale yellow and smooth, about 3 minutes. Set aside.

In a small saucepan, heat the milk and cream over medium heat. When small bubbles start to appear on the edge of the pan and the mixture is steaming, it's warm enough. Slowly stream a portion of this mixture into the egg yolk mixture. Constantly whisk to keep the egg yolks from curdling. Once half of the warm milk mixture is incorporated into the eggs, pour the entire mixture back into the saucepan.

Bring the mixture to a simmer over medium heat, about 8 minutes. When it coats the back of a spoon, remove it from the heat, cover, and chill until cold.

Pour the cold mixture into the ice-cream maker, and churn according to the manufacturer's instructions. Once churned, scrape the mixture into a loaf pan and freeze for several hours until firm.

TO MAKE THE LEMON CURD: In a medium-size bowl, using an electric mixer on medium speed, beat together the butter and sugar until well combined. Add the egg and egg yolks one at a time while beating constantly. Finally, stream in the lemon juice and salt. The mixture may look a bit curdled – it's fine.

Pour the lemon curd into a small saucepan and bring to a simmer over medium-low heat to thicken. Once simmering, remove from the heat and let cool.

TO SERVE: Dollop the lemon curd into the ice cream, and swirl with a knife. Top with crushed gingersnaps and serve.

CAKES

Cupcakes, Cheesecakes, and Layer Cakes

This is quite possibly my favorite recipe in the book. I love a good, light angel food cake. And since it's light, I like to pile it with whipped cream. A few summers ago, my parents were visiting me in California. I wooed them with the best California strawberries I could find. We decided that year that angel food cake with fresh whipped cream and berries should be our go-to summer dessert. We haven't wavered since.

ANGEL FOOD CUPCAKES
with Cloud Frosting

Yield • 6 cupcakes

FOR THE CUPCAKES

¼ cup (30 grams) all-purpose flour

1 ½ teaspoons cornstarch

⅛ teaspoon salt

3 large egg whites

¼ teaspoon cream of tartar

5 tablespoons (62.5 grams) granulated sugar

¼ teaspoon vanilla extract

FOR THE CLOUD FROSTING

⅓ cup (80 mL) cold heavy whipping cream

1 tablespoon (6.5 grams) powdered sugar

¼ teaspoon vanilla extract

TO MAKE THE CUPCAKES: Preheat the oven to 350°F, and place cupcake liners in six cups of a muffin pan.

In a medium-size bowl, sift together the flour, cornstarch, and salt. Sift it back into another bowl, and repeat the process three more times to ensure it's well aerated and mixed.

In another medium-size bowl, using an electric mixer on high speed, beat the egg whites just until foamy. Add the cream of tartar and continue to beat until soft peaks form.

Slowly stream in the sugar 1 tablespoon at a time, while beating continuously. Beat in the vanilla extract.

Finally, add the flour mixture in three parts, folding it in gently with a spatula. (To fold, sweep the spatula around the edge of the bowl, and then through the center of the batter.) Repeat until well combined.

Divide the mixture among the prepared muffin cups. Bake for 16 to 18 minutes, or until a toothpick inserted into the center of a cupcake comes out clean.

Let cool near the oven (drastic temperature change causes them to shrink too quickly).

TO MAKE THE FROSTING: When the cupcakes are cool, beat the cream until soft peaks form. Add the powdered sugar and vanilla and beat until incorporated.

Frost the cupcakes and serve.

One of the first recipes that I ever scaled down. There's just something about this warm cinnamony chocolate cake with the warm icing poured on top. It's the cake of my childhood. The icing sets into the perfect soft fudge texture that keeps you going back, forkful after forkful.

MINI TEXAS CHOCOLATE SHEET CAKE

Yield • 1 (6-inch) round cake

FOR THE SHEET CAKE

Butter, for pan

½ cup (60 grams) all-purpose flour

5 tablespoons (35 grams) unsweetened cocoa powder

½ teaspoon ground cinnamon

½ teaspoon baking soda

⅓ cup (80 mL) canola oil

½ cup (100 grams) granulated sugar

⅓ cup (80 mL) full-fat sour cream

1 large egg

½ teaspoon vanilla extract

1 tablespoon (15 mL) warm water

FOR THE FUDGE FROSTING

2 tablespoons (30 mL) unsalted butter

1 tablespoon (7 grams) unsweetened cocoa powder

1 to 2 tablespoons (15 to 30 mL) buttermilk

1 cup (100 grams) powdered sugar

TO MAKE THE CAKE: Preheat the oven to 350°F and position a rack in the lower third of the oven. Line the bottom of a 6-inch round cake pan with 3-inch sides with parchment paper, and then butter the sides of the pan, too.

In a small bowl, whisk together the flour, cocoa powder, cinnamon, and baking soda. Set aside.

In a medium-size bowl, stir the oil and sugar together, using a wooden spoon. Add the sour cream, and stir until well blended. Add the egg and vanilla and stir until combined.

Sprinkle half of the dry mixture onto the wet mixture. Stir until blended. Stir in the water, followed by the remaining dry mixture. Stir until no streaks of flour remain.

Scrape the batter into the prepared pan, and bake on a cookie sheet for 30 minutes, or until a toothpick inserted into the center comes out with only moist crumbs – if you underbake, the cake will sink as it cools. Be sure to test the toothpick in several places.

Let cool in the pan for 15 minutes, and then run a knife around the edge of the pan. The cake should have shrunk away from the edges of the pan, and it should be very easy to remove.

TO MAKE THE FROSTING: In a small saucepan, combine the butter, cocoa powder, and 1 tablespoon of the buttermilk. Once everything dissolves, add the sugar and stir until thick. Add up to 1 tablespoon of buttermilk if the mixture is too thick. Immediately pour the frosting onto the warm cake. Let cool completely before serving.

>>· BERRY MINI CHEESECAKES

When you need a cheesecake quick fix, these mini cheesecakes made in muffin pans couldn't be easier. If you want to make it even faster, instead of making the crust, just drop in a small cookie wafer instead.

Yield • 4 mini cheesecakes

3 graham cracker sheets (90 grams)

6 tablespoons (75 grams) granulated sugar, divided

1 tablespoon (15 grams) unsalted butter, melted

4 whole blackberries, plus more for serving

3 ounces cream cheese, softened

1 large egg

½ teaspoon vanilla extract

½ teaspoon fresh lemon juice

PREHEAT THE OVEN TO 350°F, and place cupcake liners in four cups along the edge of a muffin pan.

In a food processor or large plastic bag, crush the graham crackers into fine crumbs. Add 1 tablespoon of the sugar and the melted butter and stir well.

Divide the crumbs among the prepared muffin cups, and use a mini shot glass to compact the crust very well. Place one blackberry on top of each crust.

In a medium-size bowl, combine the cream cheese, remaining 5 tablespoons of sugar, the egg, vanilla, and lemon juice. Beat well with an electric mixer at medium speed until combined. Pour the cheesecake mixture over the crusts. Bake for 20 minutes.

The cheesecakes will puff up and start to crack in the oven when they're done. Let cool, and then chill before serving with extra blackberries.

COCONUT CUPCAKES

Coconut cake is traditionally served around the holidays in the South. It can also make another appearance at Easter. I like it any time of year. These cupcakes are dense and rich, like mini coconut pound cakes. They make me swoon. They have turned many a coconut hater into a coconut lover. Cream cheese frosting has special powers like that.

Yield • 4 cupcakes

FOR THE CUPCAKES

¼ cup (60 mL) canola oil

⅓ cup (65 grams) granulated sugar

Pinch of salt

1 large egg, at room temperature

2 tablespoons (30 mL) unsweetened coconut milk

¼ teaspoon vanilla extract

¼ teaspoon almond extract

⅓ cup + 1 tablespoon (47.5 grams) all-purpose flour

⅛ teaspoon baking powder

⅛ teaspoon baking soda

½ cup packed (1.75 ounces) sweetened shredded coconut

TO MAKE THE CUPCAKES: Preheat the oven to 350°F. Place cupcake liners in four cups along the edge of a muffin pan.

In a medium-size bowl, using an electric mixer on medium speed, beat the oil, sugar, and salt together for at least 4 minutes, until the mixture is light and fluffy.

Add the egg, coconut milk, vanilla, and almond extract and beat for another 15 seconds.

Sprinkle the flour, baking powder, and baking soda on top of the mixture and beat just until combined—do not overmix. Finally, stir in the coconut.

Divide the batter among the prepared muffin cups (it will come almost to the top). Bake for 23 to 25 minutes, until a toothpick inserted into the center of a cupcake comes out clean. Let cool completely before frosting.

FOR THE CREAM CHEESE FROSTING

- **3 ounces cream cheese, softened**
- **2 tablespoons (30 grams) unsalted butter, at room temperature**
- **1 tablespoon (15 mL) unsweetened coconut milk**
- **⅛ teaspoon almond extract**
- **6 tablespoons (39 grams) powdered sugar, or more or less to taste**
- **½ cup packed (1.75 ounces) sweetened shredded coconut**

TO MAKE THE FROSTING: In a medium-size bowl, using an electric mixer on high speed, beat together all the frosting ingredients, except the coconut, and frost the cupcakes.

Toast the coconut in a small skillet over medium heat, stirring constantly. Remove when golden brown and use to garnish the cupcakes.

Iconic for a reason, these cupcakes are not to be missed. The thing about Red Velvet is that ever since its popularity exploded, the recipe has been muddled. A true Red Velvet cake is made with only a touch of cocoa powder and always contains buttermilk. Accept no substitutions.

My sweet friend Missy has a sweet husband who requested I make these for her birthday one year. He insisted that it wasn't a proper Red Velvet cupcake to Missy unless it had mini chocolate chips. I didn't want to sway from the classic recipe, but I decided to forge on. Once I tasted Red Velvet cupcakes with mini chocolate chips, there was no going back. They're entirely optional here — the recipe works without them — but I highly recommend them. Missy knows her cupcake stuff.

RED VELVET CUPCAKES

Yield • 4 cupcakes

FOR THE CUPCAKES

¼ cup (60 mL) canola oil

¼ cup (50 grams) granulated sugar

2 tablespoons buttermilk

1 large egg white

1 teaspoon red food coloring

⅛ teaspoon white vinegar

¼ teaspoon vanilla extract

⅓ cup + 1 (47.5 grams) tablespoon all-purpose flour

⅛ teaspoon baking soda

⅛ teaspoon salt

2 teaspoons unsweetened cocoa powder

¼ cup mini chocolate chips (optional)

FOR THE CREAM CHEESE FROSTING

3 ounces cream cheese, softened

2 tablespoons (30 grams) unsalted butter, at room temperature

6 tablespoons (39 grams) powdered sugar

1 teaspoon buttermilk

¼ teaspoon vanilla extract

TO MAKE THE CUPCAKES: Preheat the oven to 350°F. Place cupcake liners in four cups along the edge of a muffin pan.

In a medium-size bowl, using an electric mixer on medium speed, beat together the oil, sugar, buttermilk, egg white, food coloring, vinegar, and vanilla.

In another bowl, whisk together the flour, baking soda, salt, and cocoa powder.

Slowly add the dry ingredients to the wet ingredients, while mixing. Turn off the mixer and stir in the chocolate chips, if using.

Divide the batter among the prepared muffin cups. Bake for 20 to 22 minutes, or until a toothpick inserted into the center of a cupcake comes out clean. Let cool completely before frosting.

TO MAKE THE FROSTING: In a medium-size bowl, using an electric mixer on high speed, beat together all the frosting ingredients. Frost the cupcakes.

»· PUMPKIN CUPCAKES
with Bourbon Buttercream

I'm going to let you decide if these pumpkin cakes are for breakfast or dessert. Depending on that, you can call them pumpkin muffins or pumpkin cupcakes. If you're having them for breakfast, maybe leave the bourbon out of the buttercream. Maybe? Or substitute vanilla extract. If you're having them for dessert, go full on bourbon. Trust me.

Yield • 4 cupcakes

FOR THE CUPCAKES

7 tablespoons (52.5 grams) all-purpose flour

½ teaspoon baking powder

⅛ teaspoon baking soda

¼ teaspoon salt

½ teaspoon ground cinnamon

¼ teaspoon ground ginger

¼ teaspoon freshly grated nutmeg

1 large egg

½ cup (135 grams) canned pure pumpkin puree

¼ cup (45 grams) light brown sugar

3 tablespoons (37.5 grams) granulated sugar

3 tablespoons (45 mL) vegetable oil

FOR THE BOURBON BUTTERCREAM

4 tablespoons (60 grams) unsalted butter, at room temperature

1 ½ cup (150 grams) powdered sugar

2 to 3 teaspoons Bourbon whiskey

TO MAKE THE CUPCAKES: Preheat the oven to 350°F. Place cupcake liners in four cups along the edge of a muffin pan.

In a small bowl, whisk together the flour, baking powder, baking soda, salt, cinnamon, ginger, and nutmeg.

In a medium-size bowl, whisk together the egg, pumpkin puree, brown sugar, granulated sugar, and oil. Add the wet mixture to the dry mixture and stir until combined. Don't overmix.

Divide among the prepared muffin cups. Bake for 28 to 32 minutes, or until a toothpick inserted into the center of a cupcake comes out clean. Let the cupcakes cool completely before frosting.

TO MAKE THE BUTTERCREAM: In a medium-size bowl, using an electric mixer on high speed, beat together the butter and powdered sugar until fluffy, 3 to 4 minutes. Add the Bourbon and mix well. Frost the cupcakes and serve.

>>· CARROT CAKE CUPCAKES

I feel like between the months of March and April, my kitchen is flooded with carrot cakes. Between my husband requesting it for his birthday cake, and Easter fast approaching, hardly a week goes by without a carrot cake on the cake stand. These carrot cake cupcakes are a welcome addition to any springtime party.

Yield • 4 cupcakes

FOR THE CUPCAKES

3 tablespoons (45 mL) canola oil

6 tablespoons (75 grams) granulated sugar

1 large egg

½ teaspoon vanilla extract

6 tablespoons (45 grams) all-purpose flour

½ teaspoon ground cinnamon

¼ teaspoon ground ginger

⅛ teaspoon freshly grated nutmeg

⅛ teaspoon salt

¼ teaspoon baking soda

¼ teaspoon baking powder

1 tablespoon (15 mL) milk

¼ cup (24 grams) grated carrots

FOR THE CREAM CHEESE FROSTING

3 ounces cream cheese, softened

2 tablespoons (30 grams) unsalted butter, at room temperature

6 tablespoons (39 grams) powdered sugar

1 teaspoon buttermilk

¼ teaspoon vanilla extract

Walnuts, for garnish

TO MAKE THE CUPCAKES: Preheat the oven to 350°F and position a rack in the lower third of the oven. Place cupcake liners in four cups along the edge of a muffin pan.

With a wooden spoon, stir together the oil and sugar. Add the egg and vanilla and stir well.

In a small bowl, stir together the flour, cinnamon, ginger, nutmeg, salt, baking soda, and baking powder. Add half to the oil mixture, and then stir in the milk. Add the remaining flour mixture and carrots, and stir to combine.

Bake for 20 minutes, or until a toothpick inserted into the center of a cupcake comes out clean. Let the cupcakes cool completely before frosting.

TO MAKE THE FROSTING: In a medium-size bowl, using an electric mixer on high speed, beat together all the frosting ingredients. Frost the cupcakes. Garnish with walnuts.

TRES LECHES CAKE

The first year I moved to California, I met my best friend, Esther. She made me a Tres Leches cake for my birthday that year, and it's been my go-to birthday cake ever since—a soft milk cake drenched in sweet milk and topped with whipped cream. What's not to love? I hear it's great with strawberries on top, but I never have the patience to garnish the cake. I eat it straight away!

Yield • 1 (6-inch) round cake

FOR THE CAKE

Shortening or cooking spray, for pan

½ cup (2.5 ounces) unbleached all-purpose flour

¾ teaspoon baking powder

1 large egg, separated

⅛ teaspoon cream of tartar

½ cup (100 grams) granulated sugar

¼ cup (60 mL) half-and-half

TO MAKE THE CAKE: Preheat the oven to 350°F and position a rack in the middle of the oven. Grease a 6-inch cake pan.

In a small bowl, sift together the flour and baking powder. Set aside.

In a medium-size bowl, using an electric mixer with superclean beaters on high speed, whip the egg white and cream of tartar until soft peaks form. While continuing to beat, stream in the sugar about 1 tablespoon at a time. Next, beat in the egg yolk.

Fold one-third of the flour mixture into the egg white mixture, using a rubber spatula. Add 2 tablespoons of the half-and-half and other half of the egg white mixture and continue to fold. Add another third of the flour mixture, and fold in. Add the remaining 2 tablespoons of half-and-half. Finally, fold in the last of the flour mixture.

Pour the batter into the prepared cake pan. Bake for 21 to 23 minutes, or until a toothpick inserted into the center comes out clean. The cake might sink slightly in the middle, but it is fine—we're going to drench it in milks!

Let the cake cool in the pan for 10 minutes, and then run a knife around the edge of the pan to release it. Tilt the cake out upside down onto a serving plate.

FOR THE TOPPING

½ cup (120 mL) half-and-half

⅔ cup (160 mL) sweetened condensed milk

FOR THE WHIPPED CREAM FROSTING

½ cup (120 mL) heavy whipping cream

2 tablespoons (13 grams) powdered sugar

TO MAKE THE TOPPING: Whisk together the half-and-half and condensed milk. Use a toothpick to poke holes all over the cake. Drizzle the topping over the cake slowly, and let it sink in. Cover the cake and refrigerate for at least 4 hours before frosting.

TO MAKE THE FROSTING: In a medium-size bowl, using an electric mixer on high speed, whip the cream and powdered sugar together until soft peaks form. Frost the cake and serve.

The only chocolate cake recipe you'll ever need. If the mayonnaise freaks you out, just remember that mayonnaise is made of oil and eggs mixed together. Plus, almost every wedding cake you've ever eaten relied on mayonnaise to stay soft and tender. It's a baker's secret ingredient.

>>· DEVIL'S FOOD CAKE

Yield • 1 (6-inch) round cake

FOR THE CAKE

Butter, for pan

½ cup (60 grams) all-purpose flour

5 tablespoons (35 grams) unsweetened cocoa powder

½ teaspoon baking soda

⅓ cup (80 mL) canola oil

½ cup (90 grams) light brown sugar

⅓ cup (80 mL) mayonnaise

1 large egg

½ teaspoon vanilla extract

1 tablespoon (15 mL) warm brewed coffee

FOR THE FROSTING

¼ cup (60 mL) heavy whipping cream

1 cup (170 grams) semisweet chocolate chips

2 tablespoons (30 grams) unsalted butter, at room temperature

TO MAKE THE CAKE: Preheat the oven to 350°F and position a rack in the middle of the oven. Cut a 6-inch round piece of parchment paper and place it in the bottom of a 6-inch cake pan. Butter the parchment and sides of the pan.

In a small bowl, whisk together the flour, cocoa powder, and baking soda. Set aside.

In a medium-size bowl, stir together the oil and brown sugar. Add the mayonnaise and stir well. Finally, add the egg, vanilla, and coffee. Stir until well combined. Add the flour mixture and stir until well combined, but be careful not to overmix.

Scrape the batter into the prepared cake pan. Bake for 18 to 22 minutes; if you underbake, the cake will sink when cooling, so use a toothpick inserted into the center to test for doneness. Let cool completely, then slice the cake in half lengthwise to create two layers.

TO MAKE THE FROSTING: Heat the cream in a 2-cup glass measuring cup in the microwave on HIGH for 30 seconds. This should scald it. Immediately add the chocolate when it comes out of the microwave. Shake the cup gently to cover all the chocolate chips in cream, then let sit on the counter for 1 minute. Stir with a fork until the chocolate all melts and becomes shiny and smooth. Slowly add the butter, ½ tablespoon at a time, and stir until completely incorporated. Place the cup in the freezer. Stir after 10 minutes. Freeze for another 10 minutes. After 20 minutes total, the mixture should have a spreadable, frosting-like consistency. If not, keep freezing for a few minutes at a time.

Place one cake layer on a serving platter, and scoop one-third of the chocolate frosting on top. Spread evenly to the edges. Add the remaining cake layer on top, and frost the rest of the cake. It's easiest to do a thin crumb coat of frosting, then go back and frost decoratively.

MOLTEN CHOCOLATE CAKES

I've found that ramekins with slightly flared sides work best for this recipe. I use clear glass 6-ounce ramekins with flared edges, instead of straight-sided ramekins.

Yield • 2 individual cakes

Cooking spray, for ramekins

⅓ cup (56 grams) semisweet chocolate chips

4 tablespoons (60 grams) unsalted butter

3 tablespoons (37.5 grams) granulated sugar

½ teaspoon instant espresso powder

¼ teaspoon vanilla extract

1 large egg + 1 large egg yolk

2 tablespoons (15 grams) all-purpose flour

PREHEAT THE OVEN TO 425°F. Spray the ramekins liberally with cooking spray.

In a small bowl, combine the chocolate chips and butter. Microwave on HIGH in 30-second pulses, stirring between each pulse, to melt the chocolate completely.

Once the chocolate has melted, stir in the sugar, espresso powder, and vanilla. Stir for 1 minute to cool the mixture, and then stir in the egg and egg yolk. Stir until combined, and then stir in the flour.

Divide the batter between the prepared ramekins. Bake on a baking sheet for 13 to 14 minutes. The top of the cake should appear well done, but the inside will be runny.

Remove the ramekins from the baking sheet and let cool for 3 minutes before attempting to unmold. If you let the cakes cool completely in the ramekins, the cake will finish cooking all the way. To preserve the molten chocolate center, serve immediately.

FOR THE MOUSSE FROSTING

1 cup (240 mL) heavy whipping cream, divided

2 ounces (56 grams) real white chocolate (made with real cocoa butter)

1 tablespoon (6.5 grams) powdered sugar

1 thinly sliced lemon, for serving

TO MAKE THE FROSTING: Pour 3/4 cup of the cream in a medium-size bowl, place the beaters in the bowl, and refrigerate for at least 30 minutes. (This speeds up the whipping process and helps the cream stay cold when we stream in the hot chocolate later.)

Chop the white chocolate into about twenty pieces, and place in a small, heatproof bowl. In a glass measuring cup, microwave on HIGH the remaining 1/4 cup of the cream for 30 seconds, or until boiling. Be careful not to let it overflow. Immediately pour the hot cream over the white chocolate, but do not stir. Let this mixture sit for at least 2 minutes.

Remove the bowl of the cream from the fridge and, using an electric mixer on high speed, beat until soft peaks start to form. Add the powdered sugar, and beat until combined.

Whisk the white chocolate mixture until smooth and creamy—it won't take long. If this mixture isn't the consistency of pourable syrup, the chocolate got too hot and seized up. Sorry, start over.

Slowly stream the melted white chocolate into the whipped cream mixture, while beating continuously. Once the mixture is fully incorporated, frost the cake with it.

Cover and refrigerate the cake for a few hours until the mousse sets. Serve with lemon slices.

>>· OLD TIMEY PUDDING CAKES

I've heard these cakes also referred to as "magic cakes." They're magical because even though it is only one batter, during the baking process, it separates into a layer of creamy lemon pudding, a tender cake layer, and a slightly crunchy meringuelike crust. I agree it's magical to do such little effort for such impressive little cakes!

Flavor these cakes however you like: Switch out the lemon zest for other citrus, or substitute different extracts for the lemon juice.

Yield • 2 individual cakes

Unsalted butter, for ramekins

⅓ cup granulated sugar (65 grams), plus more for ramekins

1 large egg, separated

⅓ cup (80 mL) milk

1 tablespoon (15 mL) fresh lemon juice

Zest of 1 lemon

Pinch of salt

2 tablespoons (15 grams) all-purpose flour

PREHEAT THE OVEN TO 325°F. Butter and sugar two 6-ounce ramekins all the way up and slightly over the rims.

In a small bowl, using an electric mixer on medium speed, beat together the egg yolk, sugar, milk, lemon juice, and lemon zest. Add the flour and mix until combined.

Rinse the beaters. In a seperate bowl, at high speed, beat the egg white with a pinch of salt until stiff peaks form.

Using a spatula, fold the egg white into the egg yolk mixture. Once the mixture is combined, pour it into the prepared ramekins. It will fill the ramekins to the top. Place the ramekins in an 8- or 9-inch square glass baking dish.

Make a water bath for them to cook in by pouring 2 cups of very hot water into the dish, or enough to come up about ½-inch on the sides of the ramekins.

Bake for 40 to 45 minutes. The cakes are done when the tops are lightly golden brown and spring back when touched. Tip the cakes out of the ramekins immediately for serving.

If you know me well enough by now, you'll know that I included this recipe in the book just so I could brag about another Texas-born dessert. German chocolate cake has zero connections to Germany—it was created by a Texan with the last name "German" and first published in a Dallas newspaper. As if a chocolate cake with a creamy, rich filling could come from anywhere but the sweet South! My filling is a bit creamier than the average German chocolate cake filling, because I love a frosting that acts like a sauce and coats the entire slice of cake. If you prefer a more traditional filling, use less evaporated milk, and cook it slightly longer.

>> GERMAN CHOCOLATE CAKE

Yield • 1 (6-inch) round cake

FOR THE CAKE

1 recipe One-Bowl Chocolate Cake (page 130)

FOR THE COCONUT-PECAN FILLING

12 ounce (350 mL) can evaporated milk (do not use fat-free)

⅔ cup (130 grams) granulated sugar

2 large egg yolks

4 tablespoons (60 grams) unsalted butter

¼ teaspoon salt

½ cup (75 grams) chopped pecans

1 ¼ cup (150 grams) sweetened shredded coconut

TO MAKE THE CAKE: Prepare the cake according to its recipe directions.

TO MAKE THE FILLING: While the cake is cooling, whisk the evaporated milk, sugar, egg yolks, butter, and salt together in a small saucepan. Bring to a simmer over medium heat and cook, stirring continuously, for 1 minute.

Remove the pan from the heat, and stir in the pecans and coconut. Allow to cool slightly, then pour in a bowl, and press plastic wrap directly onto the surface and chill the mixture overnight. You can speed up the process by placing the pan in the freezer for about 2 hours. It will thicken quite a bit as it cools.

Slice the cake into two even layers, placing one layer on a serving dish. Scoop a small amount of frosting on top. Spread evenly to the edges. Top with the remaining cake layer and use the remaining filling to frost.

»· ITALIAN CREAM CAKE

Admittedly, this is pronounced "eye-talian" where I'm from. But pronounce it however you like, it's a classic cake for a reason. Tender vanilla cake with the perfect crumb, topped with cream cheese frosting and plenty of chopped, toasted pecans.

Yield • 1 (6-inch) round cake

FOR THE CAKE

Cooking spray

1 large egg, separated

6 tablespoons (72 grams) solid vegetable shortening

½ cup (100 grams) granulated sugar

¼ teaspoon vanilla extract

¾ cup (90 grams) all-purpose flour

⅛ teaspoon salt

¼ teaspoon baking soda

⅛ teaspoon baking powder

¼ cup (60 mL) buttermilk

¼ cup (25 grams) sweetened shredded coconut

TO MAKE THE CAKE: Preheat the oven to 350°F, and spray a 6-inch round cake pan with cooking spray.

In a small bowl, using an electric mixer on high speed, beat the egg white until stiff peaks form.

In a separate bowl, using an electric mixer on medium speed, beat together the shortening and sugar until creamy, 1 to 2 minutes. Add the egg yolk and vanilla and beat just until blended.

In a third bowl, whisk together the flour, salt, baking soda, and baking powder. Add half of the dry ingredients to the shortening mixture and beat until combined. Add 2 tablespoons of the buttermilk and continue to beat. Add the remaining dry ingredients and beat until combined. Add the remaining 2 tablespoons of buttermilk followed by the coconut. Gently fold the egg white into the batter.

Pour the batter into the prepared pan. Bake for 32–34 minutes, or until a toothpick inserted in the center comes out clean. Let cool for 10 minutes, then carefully tip the cake out of the pan onto a cooling rack.

FOR THE CREAM CHEESE FROSTING

5 ounces cream cheese, softened

2 tablespoons (30 grams) unsalted butter, at room temperature

1 ½ cup (150 grams) powdered sugar

½ teaspoon vanilla extract

½ cup (75 grams) chopped toasted pecans

TO MAKE THE FROSTING: In a medium-size bowl, using an electric mixer on high speed, beat together the cream cheese, butter, powdered sugar, and vanilla until fluffy.

Slice the cake into two even layers, placing one layer on a serving dish. Scoop a small amount of frosting on top and sprinkle with a few pecans. Spread evenly to the edges. Top with the remaining cake layer and frost. Sprinkle the rest of the pecans around the edge of the cake. Slice and serve.

EKCO
MADE IN U.S.A

MINI SOUR CREAM POUND CAKES

A slightly indulgent Sunday breakfast is a slice of pound cake right out of the toaster. And since I didn't want a daily cake-for-breakfast habit to start, I scaled down my favorite sour cream pound cake to make four little cakes instead of an entire loaf. I can eat two for breakfast on Sunday, share the others with someone I love, and then get back to healthy breakfasts Monday morning. It's a win-win.

Yield • 4 individual cakes

¼ cup (50 grams) granulated sugar

4 tablespoons (60 grams) unsalted butter, at room temperature

½ teaspoon vanilla extract

¼ teaspoon almond extract

1 large egg + 1 large egg yolk

3 tablespoons (45 mL) full-fat sour cream

½ cup (60 grams) all-purpose flour

¼ teaspoon baking powder

⅛ teaspoon salt

PREHEAT THE OVEN TO 375°F. Place cupcake liners in four cups along the edge of a muffin pan.

In a medium-size bowl, using an electric mixer on medium speed, cream together the sugar and butter for 1 minute. Add the vanilla and almond extract and beat until combined. Next, add the whole egg, egg yolk, and sour cream and beat until combined.

Sprinkle the flour, baking powder, and salt on top of the wet ingredients. Beat until just combined; do not overmix.

Divide the batter equally among the prepared muffin cups. Bake for 16 to 18 minutes. It's okay to remove the pound cakes when moist crumbs cling to a toothpick inserted into the center of a cake, and the tops appear slightly damp. Let cool in the pan for 5 minutes, and then allow to cool completely on a cooling rack.

TO MAKE THE FROSTING: Combine the butter and shortening in a large bowl. Using an electric mixer on high speed, beat until creamy. Add the vanilla and almond extract and beat well. Slowly add the powdered sugar while beating. Turn the mixer speed to high and whip for at least 1 minute to ensure a fluffy frosting.

Now, stack the cakes. I like a slightly asymmetrical cake, and chose to place the top two layers over to one side so I could decorate the other side with greenery. It's your call. Place the largest (6-inch) cake on a cake stand. Place little pieces of parchment paper underneath the edges to catch frosting drips and smears. Frost the cake, and then stack the midsize layer on top. Frost this layer, and then place the smallest layer on top and frost. Scoop the excess frosting into a bag fitted with a decorative tip and use it to decorate the edges of the cake layers.

Remove the parchment paper strips and enjoy cutting the cake with your sweetie.

CARAMEL CAKE

Caramel cake is a labor of love. Keep telling yourself this as you make the caramel frosting. It can be a bit arduous to stir a boiling pot of caramel sauce, and then again to beat it for fifteen whole minutes. But after one taste, you'll understand why this classic cake is still served. Nothing else tastes quite like it.

Yield • 1 (6-inch) round cake

FOR THE CAKE

Cooking spray or butter, for pan (optional)

3 tablespoons (45 grams) unsalted butter, at room temperature

½ cup (100 grams) granulated sugar

1 large egg white

½ teaspoon vanilla extract

½ cup + 3 tablespoons (82.5 grams) all-purpose flour

¼ teaspoon baking soda

⅛ teaspoon salt

¼ cup (60 mL) sour cream

FOR THE FROSTING

1 ½ cups (300 grams) granulated sugar, divided

2 tablespoons (15 grams) all-purpose flour

¾ cup (180 mL) whole milk

7 tablespoons (105 grams) unsalted butter

½ teaspoon vanilla extract

TO MAKE THE CAKE: First, preheat the oven to 325°F and grease a 6-inch round cake pan with cooking spray or butter.

In a medium-size bowl, using an electric mixer on medium speed, cream the butter for 30 seconds. Slowly stream in the sugar while beating. Next, add the egg white and vanilla and beat until combined.

In a small bowl, combine the flour, baking soda, and salt. Add one-third of the flour mixture to the butter mixture, and beat until combined. Add 2 tablespoons of the sour cream. Add another third of the flour mixture, and the remaining 2 tablespoons of the sour cream. Finally, add the last third of the flour mixture.

Scrape the batter into the prepared pan. Bake for 20 to 25 minutes, or until a toothpick inserted into the center comes out clean.

TO MAKE THE FROSTING: In a small saucepan, heat ¼ cup of the sugar over medium heat and, while stirring constantly. Let it melt and turn a medium caramel brown. It will clump before it melts—just keep stirring. It's important to melt the sugar slowly and not let it start to caramelize and turn brown until all of the lumps have dissolved.

Meanwhile, combine the remaining 1 ¼ cups of sugar, the flour, and the milk in a 2-quart saucepan. Bring to a simmer over medium heat, whisking every so often. It should thicken like a béchamel sauce. Once the ¼ cup of sugar is medium brown, slowly stream it into the thickened milk mixture. Be careful—it will bubble up. Clip a candy thermometer to the edge of the pan, and boil the mixture until it reaches 238°F. Remove from the heat, and add the butter, stirring until it dissolves.

Pour the hot caramel into a large glass bowl and let cool for about 45 minutes, or until it's barely warm to the touch.

Whip the cooled caramel mixture for 15 minutes with an electric mixer on high speed. Then stir in the vanilla.

Refrigerate the frosting for 5 to 10 minutes, if it's not the perfect spreading consistency.

Slice the cake into two even layers, placing one layer on a serving dish. Scoop a small amount of frosting on top. Spread evenly to the edges. Top with the remaining cake layer and frost the entire cake.

>>· PERSONAL PINEAPPLE UPSIDE-DOWN CAKES

Another excellent contender for my week-long birthday celebration. Caramelized fruit on top of a buttermilk cake always wins my heart. If you don't want to buy a jar of maraschino cherries just for this cake, you can leave them out entirely, or substitute a beautiful pecan half.

Yield • 2 individual cakes

FOR THE PINEAPPLE TOPPING

2 tablespoons (30 grams) unsalted butter, plus more for ramekins

2 teaspoons granulated sugar

3 tablespoons (34.5 grams) light brown sugar

4 pineapple rings from an 8-ounce can (usually each can has only 4 slices)

1 halved maraschino cherry

FOR THE CAKES

3 tablespoons (45 grams) unsalted butter, at room temperature

2 tablespoons (13 grams) + 2 teaspoons granulated sugar

½ teaspoon vanilla extract

¼ teaspoon almond extract

1 large egg

½ cup (60 grams) all-purpose flour

Pinch of salt

¾ teaspoon baking powder

⅓ cup (80 mL) buttermilk

TO MAKE THE TOPPING: Preheat the oven to 350°F and butter and sugar two 10-ounce ramekins with 1 teaspoon of granulated sugar each.

In a small skillet over medium-low heat, melt the brown sugar and 2 tablespoons butter. When the sugar is melted, divide the mixture between the two ramekins.

Place one pineapple ring in the center of each ramekin. Slice up the remaining rings and arrange them around the whole ring to cover the entire bottom of the ramekin. Place one cherry half in the center of each middle ring, with the flat part facing down. Set aside while making the cake batter.

TO MAKE THE CAKES: In a medium-size bowl, using an electric mixer on medium speed, beat together the butter and sugar. Add the vanilla and almond extract, then the egg, mixing well. Add the flour, salt, and baking powder. Beat well. Finally, beat in the buttermilk.

Divide the batter evenly between the prepared ramekins. Bake for 30 minutes.

Let cool for 10 to 15 minutes before inverting onto plates.

>>· BANANA SPLIT CHEESECAKES

It's a really good thing this recipe makes two individual cheesecakes and not one to share, because I can never share cheesecake!

Yield • 2 (4½-inch) round cakes

4 graham cracker sheets (120 grams)

2 tablespoons (30 grams) unsalted butter, melted

½ cup (100 grams) + 2 teaspoons granulated sugar, divided

8 ounces cream cheese, softened

1 small banana, mashed (2 ounces total)

1 large egg

2 large strawberries (2 ounces total), hulled and diced

2 tablespoons (30 mL) chocolate sauce, plus more for serving

Whipped cream, for serving

Extra strawberries, for serving

PREHEAT THE OVEN TO 350°F. Have ready two 4 ½-inch mini cheesecake springform pans with removable bottoms.

In a food processor or large plastic bag, crush the graham crackers. Add the melted butter and 2 teaspoons of the sugar and stir to combine.

Divide the crumbs between the prepared pans, pressing them firmly on the bottom and sides of the pans.

Bake the crusts for 7 minutes. After baking, remove the crusts, crack open the oven door, and lower the temperature to 300°F.

In a large bowl, using an electric mixer on medium speed, beat together the remaining ½ cup of sugar with the cream cheese, banana, and egg. Beat very well until homogenous. Pour one-fourth of this mixture into each awaiting crust. Divide the strawberries and sprinkle evenly on top of the cheese mixture. Next, drizzle on the chocolate sauce evenly. Swirl it in with a knife, if desired. Finally, add the remaining cheesecake batter to the pans, and place them on a small baking sheet.

Bake for 30 minutes, or until set in the middle. Let cool completely in the pans, and chill overnight for best flavor. To serve, top with whipped cream, extra chocolate sauce, and strawberries.

My beautiful niece has to share her birth month with her two brothers. I can't imagine a worse plight for a middle sister. And while her brothers want all sorts of chocolate cakes covered in chocolate frosting and topped with more chocolate, all Kennedi wants is a sweet, pink strawberry cake. So, this cake is just for Kennedi. I make the cake in an 8-inch square pan because when sliced in half and stacked with strawberry cream frosting, you end up with two generous portions of a two-layer cake. Now that's a cake she won't have to share with her pesky brothers at all!

STRAWBERRY CAKE FOR KENNEDI

Yield • 1 (8-inch) square cake

FOR THE CAKE

1 cup (200 grams) granulated sugar

7 tablespoons (105 grams) unsalted butter, at room temperature

2 large eggs

1 teaspoon vanilla extract

1 cup (120 grams) all-purpose flour

1 ½ teaspoons baking powder

⅓ cup (80 mL) milk

1 cup (5 ounces) strawberries, hulled and diced small

FOR THE FROSTING

4 ounces cream cheese, softened

3 tablespoons (45 grams) unsalted butter, at room temperature

1 cup (100 grams) powdered sugar

4 strawberries, hulled and minced

TO MAKE THE CAKE: Preheat the oven to 325°F, and grease an 8-inch square baking pan. Line the bottom of the pan with a square of parchment paper.

In a medium-size bowl, using an electric mixer on medium speed, beat together the sugar and butter until light and fluffy, 1 to 2 minutes. Add the eggs and vanilla, and beat until combined.

In a small bowl, whisk together the flour and baking powder. Sprinkle half over the batter, and stir until combined. Add half of the milk and stir again. Repeat with the remaining flour and milk. Finally, stir in the strawberries.

Bake for 28 to 32 minutes, or until a toothpick inserted into the center comes out clean.

Let cool completely in the pan on a cooling rack, then run a knife around the edge and flip the cake out. Peel off the parchment paper.

Cut the cake in half evenly down the middle, and set aside.

TO MAKE THE FROSTING: Make the frosting no more than an hour before you plan to serve the cake, as the strawberries start to weep in the sugar.

In a medium-size bowl, using an electric mixer on high speed, beat together all the ingredients for the frosting until light and fluffy.

Place a cake half on a serving platter, and top with a bit of the frosting. Stack the other half on top, and frost the entire cake.

Slice the cake in half for two big perfect squares of birthday cake! Serve with extra strawberries on top.

>>· HOT FUDGE SUNDAE CUPCAKES

Make these for your best friend, make these for your partner, make these for your face. I haven't found a problem that these puppies couldn't solve.

Yield • 4 cupcakes

⅓ cup (40 grams) all-purpose flour

2 tablespoons (14 grams) unsweetened cocoa powder

¼ teaspoon baking soda

¼ teaspoon baking powder

¼ teaspoon instant espresso powder

4 teaspoons (20 mL) neutral oil, such as canola

½ teaspoon vanilla extract

¼ cup (45 grams) lightly packed light brown sugar

⅓ cup (80 mL) buttermilk

4 scoops of your favorite ice cream, for serving

Freshly whipped cream (or a can of it!), for serving

Hot fudge sauce, for serving

Colorful sprinkles, for serving

Maraschino cherries, for serving

PREHEAT THE OVEN TO 350°F. Place cupcake liners in four cups along the edge of a muffin pan.

In a medium-size bowl, whisk together the flour, cocoa powder, baking powder, baking soda, and espresso powder. Set aside.

In a small bowl, whisk together the oil, vanilla, brown sugar, and buttermilk. Add the wet ingredients to the dry, and stir to combine.

Divide the batter evenly among the prepared muffin cups. Bake for 14 to 17 minutes, or until a toothpick inserted into the center of a cupcake comes out with only moist crumbs clinging to it. Remove from the oven, and remove the cupcakes from the pan. Let cool completely.

Before serving, place one scoop of ice cream on top of each cupcake. Top with whipped cream, hot fudge sauce, sprinkles, and cherries. Dig in!

WARM BROWNIE SUNDAE

I like to end a Friday date-night-at-home dinner with this easy dessert. But, really, it's great for putting a pep back in your step on a lousy Monday, too. Use your favorite flavor of ice cream on top. I'm partial to chocolate chip, but mint chip is frequently perched on top of this brownie in my house, too.

Yield • 1 (6-inch) round cake

Cooking spray

4 tablespoons (60 grams) unsalted butter

½ cup (100 grams) granulated sugar

¼ cup + 2 tablespoons (42 grams) unsweetened cocoa powder

¼ teaspoon salt

½ teaspoon vanilla extract

1 large egg

¼ cup (30 grams) all-purpose flour

2 tablespoons (23 grams) semisweet chocolate chips

1 scoop of your favorite ice cream

Heavy whipped cream (optional)

1 Maraschino cherry (optional)

PREHEAT THE OVEN TO 325°F, and spray a 6-inch cast-iron skillet (or other ovenproof small skillet) with cooking spray.

Dice the butter into eight pieces and place in a microwave-safe bowl. Sprinkle the sugar and cocoa powder on top. Microwave on HIGH for 30 seconds. Stop, stir, and then microwave for another 30 seconds.

Carefully remove the bowl from the microwave, and stir in the salt and vanilla. Stir for about 30 seconds to cool the mixture. Then, add the egg and stir well.

Sprinkle the flour on top, and then stir vigorously for fifty strokes, using a wooden spoon. The brownie batter will become thick and glossy. Finally, stir in the chocolate chips.

Scrape the mixture into the prepared skillet. Bake for 24 to 28 minutes. It's okay for the brownie to stay a little gooey in the middle.

Top with the ice cream, whipped cream, and a cherry and serve immediately with two spoons.

>>· MINI JELLY ROLL

I'm not sure why the simple jelly roll cake has fallen out of favor. It was my grandmother's favorite cake, and very common in her day. I think it's because the cake comes together with simple pantry items. Just pop a jar of your favorite jam (I go gaga for plum preserves), roll it up in the cake, slice, and serve. Don't be scared of rolling the cake. The batter is spongy and meant to be rolled. Just work quickly, using foil to help you as you go.

Yield • 1 (8-inch-long) jelly roll

5 tablespoons (37.5 grams) all-purpose flour

½ teaspoon baking powder

½ teaspoon cornstarch

3 tablespoons (45 mL) milk (I use 2%)

1 tablespoon (15 grams) unsalted butter

5 tablespoons (62.5 grams) granulated sugar

2 large eggs, at room temperature

⅓ cup favorite jam (I use raspberry or plum)

Powdered sugar, for serving

PREHEAT THE OVEN TO 350°F.

Use an 8-inch square baking pan with sharp corners for this recipe; I don't recommend ceramic bakeware because the edges are rounded, and the cake won't roll evenly. Trim parchment paper to fit the bottom of the pan perfectly by flipping the pan over and tracing the bottom of the pan onto the paper. Place the parchment in the bottom of the brownie pan. Do not grease the pan.

In a medium-size bowl, sift together the flour, baking powder, and cornstarch twice. Be careful not to lose any of the flour in the transfer.

Melt the butter into the milk in a small microwave-safe dish in the microwave, about 20 seconds on HIGH. Set aside.

In a medium-size bowl, combine the granulated sugar and eggs. Beat with an electric mixer on high speed until it has the consistency of softened whipped cream. This can take anywhere from 5 to 10 minutes.

Add one-third of the flour mixture to the egg mixture. Using a rubber spatula, gently fold the mixture together. (Slice down the middle with the spatula, and then sweep the sides of the bowl.) Add another third of the flour mixture, and repeat the folding process. Take your time; don't rush it. Finally, add the remaining flour and fold in very well.

Reheat the butter mixture for 15 seconds in the microwave, until steamy hot. Pour all of it at once into the flour mixture and fold it together.

Scrape the batter into the prepared pan. Bake for 20 minutes, or until a toothpick inserted in the center comes out clean.

Remove the pan from the oven, and let it cool on a cooling rack for 10 minutes. After 10 minutes, run a butter knife around the edges of the cake to release it from the pan, and then gently tip the cake out onto the cooling rack, bottom facing up.

Let the cake cool completely before gently peeling off the parchment paper. A slight coating of cake may stick to it—it's fine.

Once the cake has completely cooled, transfer the cake to a piece of aluminum foil. Beginning with the edge closest to you, roll the first inch of the cake tightly and firmly. Squeeze the roll together all along the edges with your hands, and use the foil to keep rolling up the cake. The foil will stay on the outside of the cake, but it will help you roll it tightly. When you get to the end, squeeze the cake roll together in your hands to ensure a tight roll. Twist the ends of the foil closed, and refrigerate the cake for at least 4 hours. You could do this 1 day in advance.

Before serving, unroll the cake gently, and spread it with the jam. Roll it back up, sprinkle with powdered sugar, slice, and serve.

SOUTHERN DELIGHTS

Pies, Cobblers, and Puddings

TEXAS PEACH COBBLER

Texas peach season is the best time of the year. This is not debatable. If you eat peaches that don't drip juice down your chin and all the way down to your elbows, consider yourself deprived. Since we can't all live in the great state of Texas, seek out a local source of peaches and make sure they smell stronger than your grandma's perfume before attempting to eat them. Then, pile them in this cobbler. This cobbler recipe is a bit different than what you're probably used to — we're going to melt the butter in the oven, add a pancakelike batter, and finally add the peaches on top — all without stirring. Don't you stir this one bit!

Yield • 2 individual pies

2 tablespoons (30 grams) cold unsalted butter

3 ripe peaches (1 pound whole peaches)

¼ cup (50 grams) granulated sugar, divided

1 teaspoon fresh lemon juice

¼ teaspoon ground cinnamon

¼ teaspoon vanilla extract

5 tablespoons (37.5 grams) all-purpose flour

½ teaspoon baking powder

¼ cup (60 mL) half-and-half

PREHEAT THE OVEN TO 350°F. While the oven is preheating, place 1 tablespoon of the butter in each of two 10-ounce ramekins. You can also bake this in a small baking dish that holds 4 cups. Place the ramekins in the oven while it preheats, but keep an eye on it – don't let the butter brown.

Meanwhile, peel, halve, and pit the peaches. Using a spoon, scrape the center of each peach to remove the reddish center – it becomes bitter when baked. Then, slice each peach into about eight slices. Stir together the peaches, 1 tablespoon of the sugar, and the lemon juice, cinnamon, and vanilla in a bowl and set aside while you make the batter.

Whisk together the flour, the remaining 3 tablespoons of sugar, and the baking powder. Lightly stir in the half-and-half – small lumps are okay.

Spoon this mixture over the melted butter in the baking dish and *do not stir*. Evenly pour the fruit on top.

Bake for 30 to 35 minutes, or until the crust is golden brown.

BLACKBERRY COBBLER
with Lemon Biscuits

A warm berry cobbler with lemony biscuits on top. Yep, it's exactly as delicious as it sounds.

Yield • 1 small cobbler

FOR THE FILLING

12 ounces unsweetened frozen blackberries

¼ cup (50 grams) granulated sugar

1 ½ teaspoons fresh lemon juice

¼ teaspoon ground cinnamon

2 tablespoons (15 grams) all-purpose flour

FOR THE LEMON BISCUITS

⅔ cup (80 grams) all-purpose flour

1 ½ teaspoons baking powder

½ teaspoon kosher salt

1 teaspoon granulated sugar

½ cup (120 mL) heavy whipping cream

Zest of 1 lemon

1 egg yolk, beaten (optional)

TO MAKE THE FILLING: Preheat the oven to 400°F.

Place the blackberries in a small baking dish with a 3- to 4-cup capacity. Sprinkle the sugar, lemon juice, cinnamon, and flour on top. Stir gently to combine.

TO MAKE THE BISCUITS: Combine the flour, baking powder, salt, and sugar in a bowl. Make a well in the center, then pour in the cream and add the lemon zest. Knead until a dough comes together.

Pat the dough into a 6-inch square, and then cut it into nine squares. Scatter the dough pieces on top of the blackberries. Brush the dough with the beaten egg yolk, if using.

Bake for 20 minutes, until the berries are bubbling and the biscuits are browned. Serve warm.

BLACK-BOTTOM PEANUT BUTTER PIE

If chocolate and peanut butter don't hurry up and get married already, I don't know what I'm going to do. They are so clearly made for each other. This creamy peanut butter pie with a secret chocolate layer is the stuff of which dreams are made.

Yield • 1 (6-inch) pie

3 graham cracker sheets (90 grams)

2 tablespoons (19 grams) unsalted, roasted peanut halves

¼ cup (50 grams) + 2 teaspoons granulated sugar, divided

Pinch of salt

2 ½ tablespoons (37.5 grams) unsalted butter, melted

½ cup (95 grams) chocolate chips

2 tablespoons (14 grams) cornstarch

½ cup (120 mL) heavy whipping cream, divided

¾ cup (180 mL) milk

½ teaspoon vanilla extract

¼ cup (67.5 grams) creamy peanut butter

2 teaspoons powdered sugar

Extra peanuts, for garnish

PREHEAT THE OVEN TO 350°F, and have ready a 6-inch pie pan.

In a food processor, combine the graham crackers, peanuts, 2 teaspoons of the granulated sugar, and salt. Pulse until finely ground. Alternatively, you could crush everything in a plastic bag. Next, add the melted butter. Pulse the food processor to combine.

Press the crumbs into bottom of the pie pan and halfway up the sides, and bake on a small sheet pan for 12 minutes.

When the piecrust comes out of the oven, distribute the chocolate chips over the bottom.

Meanwhile, combine the remaining ¼ cup of granulated sugar and cornstarch in a small bowl. Slowly stream in ¼ cup of the cream while constantly whisking. Once everything is fully dissolved, slowly add the milk while whisking. Pour the mixture into a small saucepan.

Cook over medium heat until the mixture comes to a simmer and thickens. It should have a consistency like runny pudding.

Remove from the heat, and stir in the vanilla and peanut butter. Pour this mixture over the chocolate chips in the piecrust.

Let set in the fridge for at least 4 hours. I don't cover mine because I like the bit of skin that forms, but if you'd rather not have a skin on top, press plastic wrap directly on the surface of the pie before refrigerating.

Before serving, in a medium-size bowl, using an electric mixer on high speed, beat the remaining ¼ cup of cream until soft peaks form. Beat in the powdered sugar. Spread over the pie, and garnish with the extra peanuts.

»· BLUEBERRY MASON JAR LID PIES

Mini pies are fun to serve and eat, but making them can be a bit tedious. I use the lids of mason jars as a makeshift spring form pan. The pies are perfectly portioned and pop out immediately.

Yield • 2 individual pies

¾ cup (90 grams) + 2 teaspoons all-purpose flour, divided, plus more for rolling

¼ teaspoon salt

3 tablespoons (45 grams) cold unsalted butter

¼ teaspoon cider vinegar

2 to 3 tablespoons (30 to 45 mL) ice water

½ cup frozen blueberries

½ teaspoon fresh lemon zest (optional)

1 teaspoon fresh lemon juice

1 tablespoon (12.5 grams) granulated sugar

1 large egg yolk, beaten

Sanding sugar (optional)

YOU WILL NEED TWO WIDE-MOUTH MASON JAR LIDS for this recipe. You can substitute four regular-sized mason jar lids. Turn the mason jar lid inserts down so that the rubber part is down. You want to cook the pies on the metal side.

To make the crust, in a small bowl, stir together the ¾ cup of flour and the salt with a fork. Cube the butter into twelve chunks. Add six chunks of butter to the flour mixture and stir gently, and then add the remaining six butter chunks.

Use your fingertips to cream the butter into the flour. Pinch and smear the butter between your fingertips until it's very well incorporated and smaller than peas. The dough will clump when you squeeze it in your hands.

Stir the vinegar into 2 tablespoons of the ice water. Add this to the dough, and stir with a fork. The dough will easily come together into a mass. If the dough still feels too dry, add the extra tablespoon of water. Scoop the dough out onto a piece of plastic wrap, shape it into a disk, and store it wrapped in the fridge for 30 minutes. (If you store the dough for longer than 30 minutes, let it warm up before rolling or it will crack during rolling.)

Preheat the oven to 350°F and line a small sheet pan with parchment paper.

Stir the blueberries, lemon zest, lemon juice, granulated sugar, and remaining 2 teaspoons of flour together in a small bowl. Set aside while you roll out the dough.

Bring the dough out of the fridge, and lightly flour a work surface. Place the dough in the center of the flour, and then flour the top of the dough. Begin gently rolling the dough out away from you, making a quarter-turn clockwise after every two rolls. This method keeps the dough from sticking to the counter and also creates a perfect circle.

When you have a circle large enough for four mason jar lids, you're ready. Place one mason jar lid ring on the pastry and use a knife to cut a circle of dough ¼ inch larger than the lid. Repeat to make two disks. These are the piecrust bottoms. Then, use the mason jar lid top (not the ring) to cut out two pie tops.

Gently move the piecrust bottoms to the mason jar lids, and press it into place. Scoop half of the blueberry mixture onto each. Top the blueberry mixture with the pie tops. Brush beaten egg yolk very generously on each mini pie. Sprinkle with sanding sugar, if desired.

Bake for 35 to 37 minutes, or until the filling is bubbling and the crust is brown.

Let cool for 5 minutes. To serve, run a knife along the edge of the mason jar ring to release the pies.

CHOCOLATE CARAMEL MASON JAR LID TARTS

Maybe there are a lot of mason jar recipes in this book, but I just can't help it. I think they're adorable, and perfect for portion control. Ever since I noticed they mimic little tart pans with removable bottoms, I've been baking up all sorts of treats in them. Play around with the fillings in this recipe — substitute a different type of chocolate if you like, use jam instead of caramel, or try cookies instead of graham crackers. The possibilities are endless and delicious!

Yield • 4 individual tarts

4 graham cracker sheets (106 grams), broken into pieces

2 teaspoons granulated sugar

2 ½ tablespoons (37.5 grams) unsalted butter, melted

2 cups (380 grams) milk chocolate chips

¼ cup (60 mL) heavy whipping cream

2 to 3 teaspoons Salted Caramel Sauce (page 26)

PREHEAT THE OVEN TO 350°F. Place four pint-sized mason jar rings on a small baking sheet. Place the lids with the rubber part facing down.

In a food processor, combine the graham crackers and sugar. Pulse for about 30 seconds, or until finely ground. Stream in the melted butter and continue to pulse. The mixture should appear like wet sand, and it should slightly clump together when squeezed in your hand. If you overmix, it will turn into dough—not good.

Divide the graham cracker crumbs between the mason jar lids. Use a shot glass to pack in the crumbs and push them up the sides of the ring.

Bake for 10 minutes. Let cool completely on a cooling rack.

Now we're going to melt the chocolate. It can be finicky, so this is the way I do it: Bring 1 cup of water to a boil in a small saucepan. Make sure you have a glass bowl that fits over the pan without touching the water. Place the chocolate chips and cream in the glass bowl, and have it ready next to the stove. Once the water boils, turn off the heat and place the bowl of chocolate and cream over the pan. Stir, stir, stir until the chocolate melts. You may have to turn the heat back on to boil the water again, but I find that if I'm patiently daydreaming while stirring the chocolate, it all melts just fine.

Pour the melted chocolate into the tart shells. Tap the lids gently to get rid of any air bubbles. Let sit for 10 minutes.

Dot drops of caramel sauce onto the surface of the chocolate, and after a few seconds, run a toothpick or knife through the chocolate to swirl it together.

I recommend refrigerating the tarts for a few hours to set the chocolate. However, before serving, let them come back to room temperature—the chocolate is too hard when cold.

The tarts will keep for up to 3 days refrigerated.

Buttermilk pie is a comforting vanilla custard pie with the tang of buttermilk. I don't think I could ever tire of it. It's great in the summertime with fresh strawberries, and lovely in the winter with warm, poached fruit. But don't relegate it to dessert only — it's lovely for breakfast with chicory coffee, too.

›› BUTTERMILK PIE

Yield • 1 (6-inch) pie

1 recipe Classic Single Piecrust (page 145)

1 tablespoon (7.5 grams) all-purpose flour, plus more for rolling

½ cup (100 grams) granulated sugar

1 large egg

⅓ cup (80 mL) buttermilk

3 tablespoons (45 grams) unsalted butter, melted

Zest of ½ lemon

1 tablespoon (15 mL) fresh lemon juice

½ teaspoon vanilla extract

Whipped cream, for serving (optional)

PREPARE THE PIECRUST through step 1 of the directions on page 145.

Preheat the oven to 350°F.

Roll out the dough on a floured surface until it is a few inches wider than the 6-inch pie pan. Place the dough in the pie pan, fold under the edges, and crimp them decoratively.

In a medium-size bowl, stir together all the remaining ingredients, except the whipped cream. Pour into the crust. Bake for 30 to 35 minutes – the edges will be set but the middle will have a slight jiggle – it will thicken as it cools.

I like this pie chilled, so I chill it for at least 4 hours before serving with whipped cream.

The first time I had this pie-cheesecake-cobbler mash-up was in apple-picking country outside Lake Tahoe, California. Esther (the same girl who makes me Tres Leches cake for my birthday) led a girls' adventure one weekend, when we picked apples, drank cider, and ate too much pie. I can't tell you a thing about the apples that day, all I remember is this cheesecake tucked into a piecrust topped with apples and crumb topping.

CARAMEL APPLE CHEESECAKE PIE

Yield • 1 (6-inch) pie

1 recipe Classic Single Piecrust (page 145)

All-purpose flour, for rolling

FOR THE CRUMB TOPPING

¼ cup (30 grams) all-purpose flour

2 teaspoons granulated sugar

¼ teaspoon ground cinnamon

Pinch of freshly grated nutmeg

⅛ teaspoon ground ginger

3 tablespoons (45 grams) unsalted butter, at room temperature

FOR THE FILLING

1 small apple (I prefer Honeycrisp)

¼ teaspoon ground cinnamon

1 teaspoon all-purpose flour

Pinch of salt

Pinch of orange zest

6 ounces cream cheese, softened

½ teaspoon vanilla extract

1 large egg, at room temperature

¼ cup (50 grams) granulated sugar

2 teaspoons cornstarch

TO SERVE

Salted Caramel Sauce (page 26)

PREPARE THE PIECRUST through step 1 of the directions on page 145.

Preheat the oven to 375°F.

TO MAKE THE TOPPING: Combine all the ingredients, except the butter, in a small bowl. Mix well. Then, add the butter and mix until well incorporated. Set aside.

TO MAKE THE FILLING: Peel, core, and dice your apple into ¼-inch chunks. You should end up with about 1 cup of diced apple.

Place the apple in a medium-size bowl and toss with the cinnamon, flour, salt, and orange zest.

In another bowl, beat together the cream cheese, vanilla, egg, sugar, and cornstarch. Set aside while you prepare the piecrust.

Roll out the dough on a floured surface until it is a few inches wider than the 6-inch pie pan. Place the dough in the pie pan, fold under the edges, and crimp them decoratively.

Transfer the pie to a small baking sheet and bake in the oven for 10 minutes.

Remove from the oven. If the crust has puffed up, gently push it back down before pouring the cream cheese mixture on top. Add the apple mixture on top, followed by the crumb topping. Bake for 30 to 40 minutes. If the crumbs aren't brown enough, broil for a few minutes. This pie is great at room temperature, or even chilled.

TO SERVE: Serve with caramel sauce.

»· STRAWBERRY SHORTCAKES

It's just not summertime if you don't bake some biscuits, and stuff them with sweet strawberries and cream. The shortcake recipe is just my basic small-batch biscuit recipe with a touch more sugar. I favor the heavy cream biscuit method because it can't fail. The biscuits always rise high with the flakiest of layers.

Yield • 2 shortcakes

FOR THE SHORTCAKES

⅔ cup (80 grams) all-purpose flour, plus more for rolling

1 ½ teaspoons baking powder

½ teaspoon salt

1 teaspoon granulated sugar

½ cup (120 mL) heavy whipping cream

1 large egg white, beaten

Coarse sugar (optional)

FOR ASSEMBLY

4 strawberries

2 teaspoons granulated sugar

3 tablespoons (45 mL) cold heavy whipping cream

1 tablespoon (6.5 grams) powdered sugar

TO MAKE THE SHORTCAKES: Preheat the oven to 400°F, and position a rack in the center of the oven. Lightly grease a small baking sheet.

In a medium-size bowl, stir together the flour, baking powder, salt, and granulated sugar. Make a well in the center, and pour in the cream. Stir gently until a dough forms.

Flour your hands and a work surface, and pile the dough on top. Sprinkle the dough with a bit of flour, and knead it no more than five times to bring it together. Pat the dough out into a 5×4-inch rectangle. Cut the dough in half to get two shortcakes. If desired, trim the edges off the biscuits. This isn't necessary, but the biscuits rise higher and won't spread as much in the oven if you do this.

Place the biscuits on the baking sheet, and brush the tops with the beaten egg white. Sprinkle with coarse sugar, if using. Bake for 12 minutes.

TO ASSEMBLE: Hull and slice the strawberries and sprinkle them with the granulated sugar. Let the berries sit until the biscuits cool completely.

Just before serving, whip together the cream and powdered sugar.

Slice each biscuit in half, fill with strawberries, and top with whipped cream.

VANILLA PUDDING

If you can master this basic vanilla pudding recipe, then you can make a butterscotch, chocolate, and coconut versions easily, with just a few substitutions.

Yield • 2 servings

½ cup (100 grams) granulated sugar

2 tablespoons (14 grams) cornstarch

½ cup (120 mL) heavy whipping cream

1 ¼ cup (300 mL) whole milk

1 large egg yolk

¼ teaspoon salt

1 teaspoon vanilla extract

1 tablespoon (15 grams) unsalted butter

COMBINE THE SUGAR AND CORNSTARCH in a medium-size bowl. Slowly whisk in the cream, followed by the milk. Pour the mixture into a small saucepan and cook over medium heat, stirring continuously, until the mixture starts to bubble around the edges and thickens. Turn off the heat.

Place the egg yolk in a small bowl. While stirring constantly, slowly add about ½ cup of the pudding, then pour this mixture back into the saucepan. Over medium heat, and stirring constantly, bring the mixture to a simmer and let simmer for 1 minute.

Turn off the heat, and stir in the vanilla and butter. Stir until the butter melts, and then pour the mixture into a bowl, cover with plastic wrap directly on the surface of the pudding, and chill for 4 hours. Serve in two small bowls.

>>· COCONUT CREAM PIE

With just a small variation on vanilla pudding and a piecrust, we have coconut cream pie!

Yield • 1 (6-inch) pie

1 recipe Classic Single Piecrust (page 145)

All-purpose flour, for rolling

FOR THE FILLING

½ cup (100 grams) granulated sugar

2 tablespoons (14 grams) cornstarch

½ cup (120 mL) heavy whipping cream

1 ¼ cup (300 mL) whole milk

1 large egg yolk

¼ teaspoon salt

¼ teaspoon almond extract

1 tablespoon (15 grams) unsalted butter

PREPARE THE PIECRUST through step 1 of the directions on page 145.

Preheat the oven to 375°F.

Roll out the dough on a floured surface until it is a few inches wider than the 6-inch pie pan. Place the dough in the pie pan, fold under the edges, and crimp them decoratively.

Transfer the pie tin to a small baking sheet. Bake for 20 minutes, until golden brown.

TO MAKE THE FILLING: Combine the sugar and cornstarch in a bowl. Slowly whisk in the cream, followed by the milk. Pour the mixture into a small saucepan and cook over medium heat, stirring continuously, until the mixture starts to bubble around the edges and thickens. Turn off the heat.

Place the egg yolk in a small bowl. Stirring constantly, slowly add about ½ cup of the pudding, then pour this mixture back into the saucepan. Over medium heat, and stirring constantly, bring the mixture to a simmer and let simmer for 1 minute.

Turn off the heat, and stir in the almond extract and butter. Stir until the butter melts, and then pour the mixture into a bowl, cover with plastic wrap directly on the surface of the pudding, and chill 4 hours.

FOR ASSEMBLY

⅓ cup (30 grams) sweetened shredded coconut

⅓ cup (80 mL) heavy whipping cream

1 tablespoon (6.5 grams) powdered sugar

TO ASSEMBLE: Before serving, toast the coconut in a dry skillet over medium heat until golden brown and fragrant. Stir often to prevent scorching.

Let the coconut cool, and then stir it into the pudding. Pour this mixture into the piecrust.

In a medium-size bowl, using an electric mixer on high speed, whip the cream until soft peaks form. Add the powdered sugar and beat until combined. Serve the pie with the whipped cream.

›› SALTED BUTTERSCOTCH PUDDING POPS

If you look closely, the only difference between this butterscotch pudding recipe and my vanilla pudding recipe is the type of sugar used. (Well, besides the heftier pinch of salt and addition of an egg yolk.) Butterscotch pudding uses brown instead of white granulated sugar. So, feel free to use this recipe for regular butterscotch pudding.

Pudding makes a great base for homemade pops — the pops are thick and creamy — never icy.

Yield • 4 pops

½ cup brown sugar

2 tablespoons (14 grams) cornstarch

¼ teaspoon salt

½ cup (120 mL) heavy whipping cream

1 ¼ cup (300 mL) milk

1 tablespoon (15 grams) unsalted butter

1 teaspoon vanilla extract

IN A MEDIUM-SIZE GLASS BOWL, combine the sugar, cornstarch, and salt. Whisk to blend.

Slowly pour in ¼ cup of the cream and whisk vigorously to dissolve the sugar and cornstarch. Add the last of the cream slowly, still whisking.

Add the milk slowly while whisking to ensure all the dry ingredients are dissolved.

Pour the mixture into a saucepan and bring the pudding to a simmer over medium heat, stirring constantly with a wooden spoon. Be sure to scrape the sides and bottom of the saucepan during cooking.

Once the pudding starts to gently simmer, lower the heat to low and cook for another minute. Turn off the heat, and then stir in the butter and vanilla.

Pour into ice pop molds and freeze overnight. Alternatively, if serving as pudding, cover with plastic wrap directly on the surface, and chill for at least 4 hours.

>>· CHOCOLATE CREAM PIE

This was the very first recipe I ever shared on my website. I chose it because it was my grandfather's favorite pie. He told us the story that when he got home from his deployment in Pearl Harbor, his sister Stacy made him this pie. He sat down at the table, and ate the entire pie in one sitting. This recipe holds all kinds of emotions for me, and I'm so happy to share it with you. I photographed the pie in my grandmother's vintage pie plate, and I can hardly keep from tearing up thinking about this pie in that pie plate. Isn't this what food is all about? Loved ones and memories?

Yield • 1 (6-inch) pie

FOR THE CRUST

4 graham cracker sheets (106 grams)

Pinch of ground cinnamon

2 teaspoons granulated sugar

2 ½ tablespoons (37.5 grams) unsalted butter, melted

FOR THE FILLING

¼ cup (50 grams) granulated sugar

3 tablespoons (21 grams) unsweetened cocoa powder

2 tablespoons (14 grams) cornstarch

½ cup (120 mL) heavy whipping cream

1 cup (240 mL) whole milk

1 teaspoon vanilla extract

1 tablespoon (15 grams) unsalted butter

FOR THE TOPPING

¼ cup (60 mL) heavy whipping cream

1 tablespoon (6.5 grams) powdered sugar

¼ teaspoon vanilla extract

TO MAKE THE CRUST: Preheat the oven to 350°F, and have ready a 6-inch pie pan.

In a food processor, pulse the graham crackers, sugar, and cinnamon until finely ground. Add the melted butter and pulse until combined. Pack the crumbs into the pie pan, and bake on a small baking sheet for 10 minutes.

TO MAKE THE FILLING: Meanwhile, combine the sugar, cocoa powder, and cornstarch in a small bowl. Whisk together very well, and then slowly stream in the cream. Once all of the dry ingredients are dissolved, whisk in the milk.

Pour the liquid into a small saucepan and cook over medium heat, stirring constantly, until the mixture comes to a simmer and thickens. It should coat the back of a spoon. Remove from the heat, and stir in the vanilla and butter.

Pour the chocolate pudding into the piecrust. Let set in the fridge for at least 4 hours. If you don't like pudding skin, press plastic wrap directly onto the surface before refrigerating.

TO MAKE THE TOPPING: Before serving, whip the cream until soft peaks form. Add the powdered sugar and vanilla, and whip until combined. Serve with the pie.

POR
DEUX
DESSERT
FOR
TWO

SWEET POTATO PIE, OH MY!

It's just not the holidays without sweet potato pie. If you're a pumpkin pie fan, it's an easy substitute in this recipe. Make sure to process the sweet potato in a food processor or through a fine sieve—lumps are the devil in this pie.

Yield • 1 (6-inch) pie

1 recipe Classic Single Piecrust (page 145)

All-purpose flour, for rolling

1 ½ cups (360 mL) sweet potato puree

2 large eggs, beaten

3 tablespoons (37.5 grams) granulated sugar

2 tablespoons (30 mL) molasses

¼ teaspoon ground cinnamon

⅛ teaspoon ground ginger

⅛ teaspoon freshly grated nutmeg

⅛ teaspoon vanilla extract

1 tablespoon (15 mL) heavy whipping cream

Whipped cream, for serving (optional)

PREPARE THE PIECRUST through step 1 of the directions on page 145.

Preheat the oven to 350°F.

Ensure the sweet potato mixture is lump free, and then mix it with all the remaining ingredients, except the whipped cream.

Roll out the dough on a floured surface until it is a few inches wider than the 6-inch pie pan. Place the dough in the pie pan, fold under the edges, and crimp them decoratively.

Pour the filling in the crust. Bake for 45 minutes. It will be slightly jiggly, but it will set as it cools.

Serve with whipped cream, if desired.

I most definitely did not grow up on rhubarb pie. In fact, I grew up with my pawpaw mowing over my meemaw's rhubarb patch, and cursing it when it grew back repeatedly. It seems rhubarb fell out of favor in my family, probably after a bumper crop year where everyone became tired of eating it. I discovered rhubarb all on my own one day at the farmers' market. How could I resist something so beautiful? Hot pink celery? Sign me up! Poisonous leaves? Whoa, there. "Just how do I cook this thing?" I asked the farmer. She rattled off a rhubarb compote recipe for topping soft cheeses. All I could think about was pie. You could use this recipe for double crust to make almost any fruit pie. You may need to increase or decrease the thickener (cornstarch), depending on the pectin levels of the fruit you're using, but you can hardly go wrong with pie.

>>· STRAWBERRY RHUBARB PIE

Yield • 1 (6-inch) pie

FOR THE DOUBLE PIECRUST

1 cup + 2 tablespoons (135 grams) all-purpose flour

2 teaspoons granulated sugar

¼ teaspoon salt

5 tablespoons (75 grams) cold unsalted butter, diced

½ teaspoon cider vinegar

4 to 5 tablespoons (60 to 75 mL) ice water

FOR THE FILLING

1 ½ cups (250 grams) fresh strawberries, hulled and diced

½ cup (60 grams) rhubarb stalks, diced

¼ cup (50 grams) granulated sugar

3 tablespoons (21 grams) cornstarch

1 large egg yolk, beaten

Coarse sugar (optional)

TO MAKE THE DOUBLE PIECRUST: In a medium-size bowl, combine the flour, sugar, and salt. Add the butter and work it into the flour mixture with your fingertips or a pastry cutter. The butter should be evenly distributed and flecked throughout the flour. Next, add the vinegar to 4 tablespoons of the ice water, and sprinkle it over the flour mixture. Stir with a fork until a dough forms. If needed, add up to 1 additional tablespoon of water until the dough comes together but isn't overly wet. Wrap in plastic wrap and let rest in the fridge for at least 30 minutes.

Preheat the oven to 425°F and position a rack in the lower third of the oven.

TO MAKE THE FILLING: In a medium-size bowl, combine the fruit with the granulated sugar and cornstarch. Set aside.

Divide the dough roughly in half, with one piece slightly larger. Roll out the slightly larger piece on a floured surface until it's a few inches larger than your 6-inch pie pan. Place it in the pan for the bottom crust, and let it hang over.

Roll out the other half of the dough for the top crust. Roll it about the same size as the pie pan.

Pour the fruit and the juices in the bottom crust, top with the top crust, and crimp the top and bottom crust together, trimming off any excess. Make a few slits in the surface of the pie for ventilation.

Brush the entire crust with the beaten egg yolk, and sprinkle with coarse sugar, if using. Bake for 20 minutes, and then open the oven to let out some of the heat. Turn the oven temperature down to 350°F, and continue to bake until the fruit starts to bubble and ooze out of the slits, about 20 minutes longer.

Let cool completely in the pan; overnight is better. Serve.

BISCUIT WHISKEY BREAD PUDDING

I'm not so sure leftover biscuits exist, but if you happen to find yourself with some, please, make this bread pudding with them. Just in case you are biscuit-less, see page 160 (strawberry shortcake biscuits) for a recipe for a small batch of biscuits so that nothing will hold you back from the deliciousness that is biscuit bread pudding with chocolate chunks and whiskey sauce. I frequently bake the biscuits the night before, slice them in half, and leave them on the counter to get a bit stale just so I can make this bread pudding. If using the recipe for biscuits from my strawberry shortcakes, just brush the tops of the biscuits with egg yolk instead of egg white for a bit more color.

Yield • 2 servings

FOR THE BREAD PUDDING

Homemade or leftover store-bought biscuits totaling 6 ounces (170 grams) by weight (about 3 cups, cubed)

2 large eggs

⅔ cup (160 mL) 2% milk

⅓ cup (80 mL) heavy whipping cream

2 teaspoons whiskey

⅓ cup (64 grams) granulated sugar

¼ cup (42 grams) dark chocolate chunks

FOR THE WHISKEY SERVING SAUCE

2 tablespoons (30 grams) unsalted butter

2 tablespoons (25 grams) granulated sugar

1 tablespoon (15 mL) whiskey

2 teaspoons heavy whipping cream, or more butter

TO MAKE THE PUDDING: Preheat the oven to 325°F, and have ready a small baking dish that holds 3 to 4 cups of liquid.

Place the biscuit cubes in the dish.

In a small bowl, whisk together the eggs, milk, cream, whiskey, sugar, and chocolate chunks. Pour over the biscuit cubes.

Bake on a small sheet pan for 25 minutes, until the top is set, and after a few pricks, no runny egg is revealed.

TO MAKE THE SAUCE: Place the butter, sugar, whiskey, and cream in a small saucepan, and warm over low heat until the butter and sugar melt.

Serve the bread pudding warm with the whiskey sauce.

>>· LEMON AMARETTO RICE PUDDING

With my dad's side of the family hailing from North Carolina, including rice pudding in this book was a no-brainer. I like my rice pudding extra creamy and extra boozy. The flavor marriage of lemon and amaretto is one that I can't quite get over. It's warm and fresh all at once.

Yield • 2 servings

1/3 cup (65 grams) long-grain white rice

2/3 cup (160 mL) whole milk

2/3 cup (160 mL) half-and-half

2 tablespoons (25 grams) granulated sugar

1 large egg yolk

1 teaspoon Amaretto liqueur

1/2 teaspoon lemon zest

1/2 teaspoon fresh lemon juice

Ground cinnamon, for serving (optional)

Sweetened whipped cream, for serving (optional)

COMBINE THE RICE, milk, and half-and-half in a medium-size saucepan. Bring to a simmer over medium low heat, cover, and cook until the rice is tender, about 20 minutes. Stir the rice halfway through the cooking time to ensure it doesn't stick to the bottom of the pan.

Meanwhile, combine the sugar and egg yolk in a small bowl.

Once the rice is cooked through, remove it from the heat, and immediately stir in the egg yolk mixture. Stir until combined and to cook the egg through. Add the amaretto, lemon zest, and lemon juice and stir.

Divide between two serving bowls and serve with cinnamon and whipped cream, if desired.

>>· APPLE PIE MOONSHINE TIRAMISU

So not your typical tiramisu. Not that there's anything wrong with the classic version of tiramisu with brandy and espresso, but apple pie moonshine and apple cider? It sounds like a Southern masterpiece to me. If mascarpone is hard to find in your area, substitute room-temperature cream cheese. If moonshine is hard to come by in your parts, use whiskey.

Yield • 2 servings

3 ounces mascarpone cheese, softened

¼ + ⅛ teaspoon ground cinnamon

¼ cup + 1 tablespoon (31.5 grams) powdered sugar, divided

⅓ cup (80 mL) heavy whipping cream

1 small Golden Delicious apple

1 tablespoon (15 mL) fresh lemon juice

½ cup (120 mL) fresh apple cider

2 tablespoons (30 mL) apple pie moonshine

12 ladyfinger cookies (about half 7-ounce package)

IN A MEDIUM-SIZE BOWL, using an electric mixer on medium speed, beat together the mascarpone cheese, cinnamon, and ¼ cup of the powdered sugar. Once incorporated, slowly add the cream while beating. Continue to beat until it has the consistency of thick whipped cream.

Using a mandoline, thinly slice the apple from one side, stopping when you hit the core. You need twelve slices total, so flip over the apple and slice the other side, too. Alternatively, you could grate the apple.

In a shallow bowl, stir together the apple cider and apple pie moonshine.

Place three apple slices (or 2 tablespoons of grated apple) in the bottom of each of two mini trifle dishes. Sprinkle the apples with a little of the lemon juice.

Quickly dip a ladyfinger in the apple cider mixture, 2 seconds per side. After dipping, slice the cookies in half to fit up the sides of the trifle dishes (see the photo for reference). Line each trifle dish with the ladyfingers, dipping more as needed.

Scoop one-quarter of the cheese mixture into each trifle dish. Top with the remaining apples and lemon juice. Finally, divide the last of the cheese mixture between the two dishes.

Cover and refrigerate for at least 5 hours before serving.

›› BANANA PUDDIN'

So quintessentially Southern, and so very necessary on Sundays. I make my banana puddings in half-pint mason jars so I can easily store them in the fridge.

Yield • 2 servings

20 vanilla wafers (such as Nilla Wafers)

1 recipe Vanilla Pudding (page 162)

1 small banana, sliced

⅓ cup (80 mL) heavy whipping cream

1 tablespoon (6.5 grams) powdered sugar

HAVE READY TWO SMALL JARS or serving dishes.

Prepare the vanilla pudding according to the recipe directions on page 162.

Layer five vanilla wafers in the bottom and up the sides of each jar. Top with a spoonful of the vanilla pudding. Top with banana slices. Repeat until the jars are full. You will have a bit of vanilla pudding left over.

Chill in the fridge for at least 4 hours.

Before serving, in a medium-size bowl, using an electric mixer on high speed, whip together the cream until soft peaks form. Add the powdered sugar, and beat until combined. Serve on top of the banana pudding.

»· MIXED BERRY CRISP

There are several holidays throughout the year when I like to pull out this beautiful red, white, and blue dessert. I happen to be married to a veteran, so Memorial Day, Veterans Day, Marine Corps Birthday, and Fourth of July are all great reasons for me to make this dessert. It relies on frozen berries, so I can enjoy it any time of year. There's just something so comforting about warm berries, crisp oats, and creamy ice cream that you can't get in any other dessert. Feel free to substitute any type of fruit you like. This is your basic fruit crisp recipe.

Yield • 2 servings

12 ounces frozen mixed berries, unthawed

2 tablespoons (25 grams) granulated sugar

4 tablespoons (30 grams) all-purpose flour, divided

1 teaspoon fresh lemon or lime juice

⅓ cup (30 grams) rolled oats

⅓ cup (60 grams) light brown sugar

3 tablespoons (45 grams) unsalted butter

¼ teaspoon vanilla extract

Vanilla ice cream, for serving

PREHEAT THE OVEN TO 375°F, and have ready a small baking dish with a 3- to 4-cup capacity.

In a medium-size bowl, stir together the frozen berries, granulated sugar, 2 tablespoons of the flour, and the lemon juice. Stir well, and set aside.

In a small bowl, combine the remaining 2 tablespoons of flour and the oats, brown sugar, vanilla, and butter. Use your fingertips to distribute the butter evenly throughout the mixture. It should be crumbly and evenly mixed.

Pour the berries and any excess flour from the bowl into the baking dish. Top with the crumble mixture. Bake for 30 to 34 minutes, or until the berries are bubbling and the top is golden brown.

Let cool in the dish for at least 15 minutes, then top with ice cream and serve.

RASPBERRY PICK-UP PIE

I call crostatas "pick-up pies." Once baked, you can cut them into four neat slices and enjoy them straight out of hand. Sometimes, a pie craving is just too strong to wait for a plate and fork.

Yield • 1 (6-inch) mini pie

½ cup (60 grams) + 2 teaspoons all-purpose flour, divided, plus more for rolling

5 teaspoons granulated sugar, divided

⅛ teaspoon salt

2 tablespoons (30 grams) cold unsalted butter, diced

¼ teaspoon white vinegar

2 to 3 tablespoons (30 to 45 mL) cold water

6 ounces (170 grams) fresh raspberries

Beaten egg yolk, for brushing

Coarse sugar (optional)

Raspberry jam, for serving (optional)

COMBINE ½ CUP OF THE FLOUR, 1 teaspoon of the granulated sugar, and the salt in a medium-size bowl. Add the butter, and work it through the dough, using two knives or a pastry blender. The butter should be smaller than peas, and evenly dispersed throughout the dough.

In a small bowl, combine the vinegar with 2 tablespoons of the cold water. Add to the dough, and stir with a fork until a shaggy dough forms. If the dough seems a bit too dry, add up to 1 additional tablespoon of water. Shape the dough into a ball, flatten into a disk, then refrigerate for at least 30 minutes.

Preheat the oven to 375°F, and place a piece of parchment paper on a small sheet pan.

Combine the raspberries, remaining 2 teaspoons of flour, and remaining 4 teaspoons of granulated sugar. Set aside.

Remove the dough from the fridge, and flour a surface on which to roll it. Roll the dough into a rough 8-inch circle. Move the dough to the sheet pan. Pile the raspberries in the center of the dough, leaving a 2-inch border all around. Begin to fold up the edges of the dough over the raspberries. The majority of the raspberries will not be covered by the crust

Brush the edges of the pie with egg yolk, and sprinkle with coarse sugar, if using.

Bake for 35 to 40 minutes. The piecrust will be shiny and golden brown, and the raspberries will slump when done.

Let cool completely before serving. I like to warm raspberry jam in the microwave and brush it on the berries before serving.

>>· BUTTERED PECAN CREAM PUFFS

Of all the desserts that I predicted would present the most challenge scaling down, I counted French profiteroles among them. Cream puffs, as we commonly call them, seem impossible. I'm happy to report they were easy to scale down to serve two. Almost a little too easy . . .

Yield • 4 cream puffs

FOR THE ICE-CREAM FILLING

2 large egg yolks

⅓ cup + 1 tablespoon (77.5 grams) granulated sugar

½ teaspoon vanilla extract

1 cup (240 mL) whole milk

1 cup (240 mL) heavy whipping cream

⅓ cup (35 grams) pecans halves

1 tablespoon (15 grams) unsalted butter

Pinch of salt

TO MAKE THE FILLING: In a small bowl, whisk together the egg yolks with the sugar until pale yellow. The mixture should fall off the whisk in sheets. It takes a few minutes of vigorous whisking. Alternately, you could use an electric hand mixer on medium speed to speed it along. Next, whisk in the vanilla.

Meanwhile, heat the milk and cream in a saucepan over medium-low heat until small bubbles form around the edges – do not boil. Slowly pour this mixture into the egg yolk mixture while whisking constantly. Once it is incorporated, pour the mixture back into the saucepan. Cook over medium heat, stirring constantly, until the mixture coats the back of a spoon. When done, pour the mixture into a bowl, cover and refrigerate until completely cold, at least 6 hours.

Freeze the ice cream mixture according to the ice cream maker's manufacturer's instructions. Meanwhile, heat the pecans, butter, and salt in a skillet over medium heat until fragrant and toasted, about 5 minutes. Let cool completely, and then stir the nuts into the ice-cream mixture after it finishes churning.

Scrape the ice-cream mixture into a freezer-safe bowl, and freeze until firm.

FOR THE CREAM PUFFS

⅓ cup (80 mL) water

3 tablespoons (45 grams) unsalted butter, at room temperature

⅓ cup (40 grams) all-purpose flour

½ teaspoon granulated sugar

⅛ teaspoon salt

1 large egg

Salted Caramel Sauce (page 26)

TO MAKE THE CREAM PUFFS: Preheat the oven to 400°F. Line a sheet pan with a silicone mat or parchment paper.

In a small saucepan, stir together the water and butter over low heat. Let the butter melt gently and try not to let the water boil.

Remove the butter mixture from the heat, and add the flour, sugar, and salt all at once. Stir, stir, stir.

You may have to leave your burner on low heat if you're cooking with gas or electric burners. If using a glass cooktop, turn it off entirely for this step. Put the pan back on its burner and stir until the dough starts to pull away from the sides of the pan. In other words, the dough will stick together in one big clump around the spoon and not the edges of the pan. It happens in about 1 minute.

Scrape the dough into a mixing bowl, and using an electric mixer on low speed, beat until the mixture is warm to the touch, 1 to 2 minutes. Add the egg and continue to beat for a few minutes, until the dough falls off the beaters in sheets and is pale yellow.

Spoon out four balls of dough, trying to pile the dough on top of itself for the highest rise during baking.

Bake for 10 minutes, open the oven door for 5 seconds, lower the oven temperature to 350°F, and close the door. Continue to bake at 350°F for 18 to 20 minutes. Do not be afraid of brownness — if you underbake, the insides will not dry out.

When the cream puffs are done baking, turn off the oven, and remove the sheet from the oven. Using a thin knife, poke a hole in the side of each puff. You will eventually cut all the way through to fill it with ice cream, but for now, just cut a slit so steam can escape. Return the pan to the turned-off oven, and let cool for 30 minutes with the oven door ajar.

TO ASSEMBLE: Slice the cream puffs in half, fill with the ice cream, and top with the caramel sauce.

I was born to fry. I love the way frying ties you to the stove, demands all of your attention and permits you to constantly poke at the food during cooking. Most of all, I love the way frying draws everyone else around the stove, too.

If you're new to frying, start here. We're only using a few cups of oil, and we're cooking in a deep pot to ensure safety.

Funnel cake batter is essentially identical to pancake batter. Actually, I halved my Buttermilk Pancakes for Two recipe from my website to create this recipe.

I recommend a squeeze bottle for dispersing the batter into the oil. And don't worry, the sides of the pan will push all the batter together, so if your batter falls in dollops instead of a stream, it will all stick together in the end.

I didn't call for an exact amount of powdered sugar. However you like your funnel cakes at the state fair as a guide.

>>· FUNNEL CAKES!

Yield • 2 funnel cakes

2 cups (475 mL) neutral-flavored oil (peanut is great)

½ cup + 1 tablespoon (67.5 grams) all-purpose flour

1 teaspoon baking powder

1 tablespoon (6.5 grams) powdered sugar, plus more for serving

Pinch of salt

½ cup (120 mL) buttermilk

1 large egg

Whipped cream, for serving

IN A 4-CUP CAPACITY SAUCEPAN, heat the oil over medium-high heat until it registers 350°F on a deep fry or candy thermometer.

In a small bowl, whisk the flour, baking powder, powdered sugar, and salt together. Add the buttermilk and egg, and whisk until combined. Transfer the batter to a squeeze bottle.

When the oil is at 350°F, gently squeeze half of the batter into the oil, dropping the batter close to the surface of the oil to minimize splashing. Cook until golden brown on one side, 30 to 45 seconds. During the cooking process, poke the funnel cake under the oil a few times so the top surface gets a quick dunk in the oil. When one side is golden brown, gently flip the funnel cake over and continue to fry another 30 seconds, or until golden brown. Remove from the oil and let rest on a paper towel to absorb excess oil. Repeat the process for the remaining batter.

Serve immediately dusted with powdered sugar and dolloped with whipped cream.

CANDY

Small Batches for a Small Sweet Tooth

HONEY BOURBON BALLS

Bourbon balls are commonly served around the holidays in the South. Homemade candy seems to fill the dessert buffet table all December long. I start making these in the fall as soon as the weather turns chilly. I replaced the usual corn syrup with honey, and I like them even better.

Yield • 8 balls

⅔ cup (56 grams/ 16 cookies) vanilla wafers (such as Nilla Wafers)

⅓ cup (42 grams) toasted pecan halves

2 tablespoons (13 grams) powdered sugar

1 tablespoon (7 grams) unsweetened cocoa powder, plus more for rolling (optional)

1 tablespoon (15 mL) honey

2 tablespoons (30 mL) honey whiskey

⅛ teaspoon vanilla extract

CRUSH THE WAFERS in a food processor or in a plastic bag, using a rolling pin. Transfer to a small bowl.

Finely chop the pecans, and add most of them to wafers, reserving the remaining nuts in a shallow bowl.

Add all the remaining ingredients, and stir until well blended.

Roll into 1 inch balls, and then roll in the reserved chopped pecans or cocoa powder, for serving.

>>· TEXAS PEANUT PATTIES

I count these chewy peanut patties as one of my favorite candies. They're so simple to make at home — all you need is a candy thermometer.

Yield • 6 patties

1 cup (200 grams) granulated sugar

1 cup raw or toasted peanuts (156 grams)

⅓ cup (80 mL) light corn syrup

2 tablespoons (30 mL) water

⅛ teaspoon salt

2 tablespoons (30 grams) unsalted butter

1 teaspoon vanilla extract

IN A DEEP, HEAVY SAUCEPAN (preferably enameled cast iron), combine the sugar, peanuts, corn syrup, water, and salt. Clip a candy thermometer to the side of the pan, but ensure the probe does not touch the bottom of the pan – you want it to hang slightly above for an accurate reading of the candy, not the pan.

Place the pan over medium heat and begin to stir the mixture with a silicone spatula. Keep stirring until the mixture reaches 240°F. Immediately turn off the heat, and add the butter and vanilla. Let the butter melt while continuing to stir, then stir every minute or so until the mixture cools to 130° to 135°F. Meanwhile, have ready a sheet of parchment or waxed paper.

Once the mixture reaches 135°F, begin to scoop it by the heaping tablespoon onto the paper. Work quickly before it sets! Press the mixture into 3- to 4-inch patties. Let cool completely on the paper, then wrap in plastic wrap for storage. Do not leave the patties uncovered – they will absorb moisture from the air and their texture will change. Keep tightly wrapped!

The minute I feel the first fall chill in the air, I make this caramel corn. My mom has been making this recipe for as long as I can remember. I halved her recipe, and stirred in the pretzels for a fun twist. Use your favorite honey, because the flavor really shines through.

PRETZEL HONEY CARAMEL CORN

Yield • About 4 cups

2 tablespoons (30 mL) neutral oil, such as canola

¼ cup (64 grams) unpopped popcorn kernels

½ cup pretzel twists

¼ cup (27 grams) chopped pecans

4 tablespoons (60 grams) unsalted butter

½ cup (90 grams) light brown sugar

3 tablespoons (45 mL) honey

⅛ teaspoon salt

¼ teaspoon vanilla extract

PREHEAT THE OVEN TO 250°F. Line a baking sheet with a silicone mat or parchment paper. Do not skip this step, or the caramel corn will stick to the pan.

In a heavy 2-quart saucepan, combine the oil and popcorn kernels. Swirl to coat all the kernels in the oil. Cover and place over high heat. Once the kernels start popping, which will take 2 to 3 minutes, shake the pan once. Leave the pan on the heat until the popping slows and almost stops. Remove the pan from the heat, and keep covered to let the final few kernels pop.

In a small saucepan, melt the butter over low heat. Add the brown sugar, honey, and salt. Bring to a rolling boil over medium-low heat. Do not stir, and let it maintain the rolling boil for 3 minutes.

When the caramel is a medium golden brown, remove the pan from the heat and allow it to cool slightly.

Meanwhile, break the pretzels into bite-size pieces and spread on the prepared baking sheet. Add the pecans and popcorn. Mix gently.

Stir the vanilla into the caramel (it will spatter a bit). Pour the caramel over the pretzels, popcorn, and pecans. Stir once, but it's okay if it's a bit too sticky to stir very well.

Bake for 15 minutes, and then stir. It should be much easier to stir now. Return to the oven for another 15 minutes. Stir. Repeat this one more time, for a total cooking time of 45 minutes.

Let the caramel corn cool on the baking sheet. Stir occasionally as it cools, to prevent large clumps (unless that's your thing). Serve when cool.

›› CHRISTMAS FUDGE

This fudge is our favorite holiday snack. We have serious pecan allergies in my family, so my mom usually leaves them off, but thankfully, I can eat them and I think they're great on top. I love this recipe because it couldn't be easier — it doesn't rely on boiling to a certain temperature. Just melt the chocolate, stir in the marshmallow cream, and you're done!

Yield • about 8 pieces of fudge

Butter, for greasing the pan

9 ounces (255 grams) semisweet chocolate chips

5 ounces (150 mL) sweetened condensed milk

3.5 ounces marshmallow cream

¼ teaspoon vanilla extract

⅓ cup (35 grams) chopped pecans, toasted

LINE A 9 × 5 × 3-INCH LOAF PAN with foil, and butter the foil generously.

In the top of a double boiler (or a bowl set over a small pan of simmering water), combine the chocolate and condensed milk over low heat. Let the chocolate slowly melt into the milk. The mixture will be thicker than regular melted chocolate.

Carefully remove the pan from the heat, and add the marshmallow cream and vanilla. Stir until no streaks of marshmallow remain.

Pack the mixture into the prepared loaf pan, and press the pecans into the surface of the fudge. Let cool in the fridge for a few hours to set up. Slice and serve.

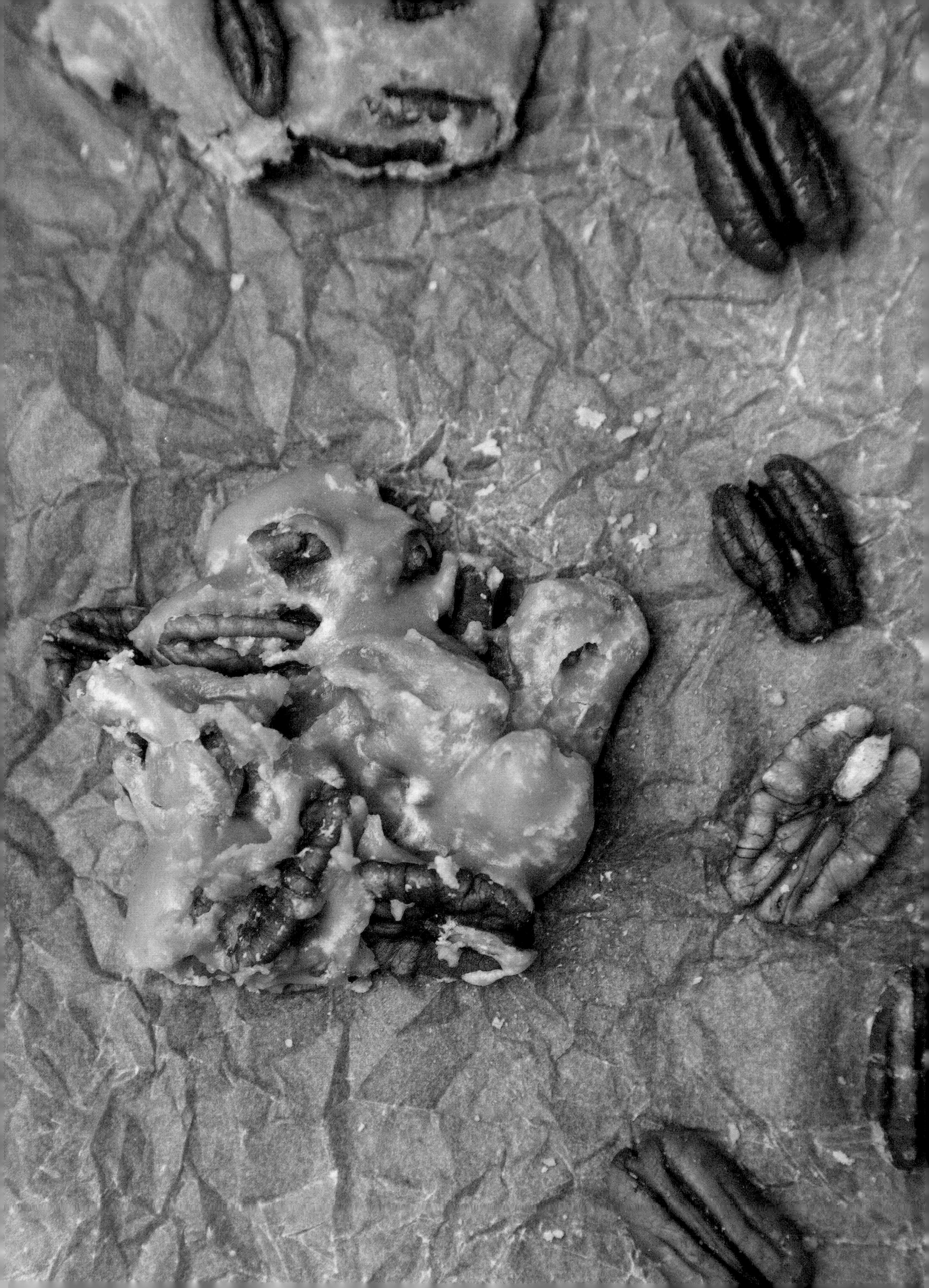

>>· PRALINES

I ate pralines on my honeymoon, so every sweet, sugary bite takes me back to New Orleans, one of the first cities on our "great Southern road trip" (a.k.a. our honeymoon), and it was easily the most memorable and moving. I learned that I will take a praline sample out of the hand of anyone who offers. I may even cross the street and do another pass by just to get another sample before finally going in the store to buy my weight in the things. There's something so pleasantly soft and ever so slightly grainy about pralines. Go ahead and make this small batch of six pralines and fall in love, too.

Yield • 6 pralines

½ cup (90 grams) light brown sugar

¼ cup (50 grams) granulated sugar

¼ cup (60 mL) water

¼ cup (60 mL) heavy whipping cream

½ cup (53 grams) toasted pecan halves

¼ teaspoon vanilla extract

HAVE READY BY THE STOVETOP A SHEET PAN lined with parchment paper.

In a medium-size saucepan, combine the brown sugar, granulated sugar, water, and cream. Bring to a boil, stirring frequently with a wooden spoon. Using a candy thermometer, bring the mixture to between 235° and 238°F.

Once up to temperature, remove the pan from the heat and, using an electric mixer on low speed, beat the mixture for 3 minutes. Be careful not to splash yourself. (Boiling things are, um, hot.)

After 3 minutes, quickly stir in the pecans and vanilla.

Drop the praline mixture into six equal-size heaps on the parchment paper sheet. Let cool to room temperature, and then eat immediately, or store in an airtight container for 2 to 3 days.

To eat divinity is to eat a sweet cloud of fluff. I've also heard it referred to as white fudge. It can be a bit dangerous to make because pouring boiling hot sugar into egg whites while beating leaves lots of room for error. Use a towel to hold the pan, and be careful not to splash the molten sugar on the sides of the mixing bowl, or it will instantly harden and not incorporate into the egg whites. That said, this recipe is positively dreamy, and great for when you want homemade candy, but don't want to be tempted with one hundred pieces of it!

I've been told by many a Southern meemaw not to make this on a humid day. If there's a day in the South that isn't humid, let me know. I make it any time of year, but I will avoid a rainy day.

>>· DIVINITY

Yield • 12 pieces divinity

1 cup (200 grams) granulated sugar

¼ cup (60 mL) water

¼ cup (60 mL) light corn syrup

⅛ teaspoon salt

1 large egg white

¾ teaspoon vanilla extract

12 pecan halves

FIRST, LINE A MINI MUFFIN PAN with twelve mini cupcake liners. Have the pecans ready nearby.

In a medium-size saucepan with high sides, combine the sugar, water, corn syrup, and salt. Stir well, but try not to splash sugar on the sides of the pan. If you do, use a pastry brush dipped in warm water to wash it back into the pan. Bring to a boil over high heat without stirring and cook until it reaches 266°F on a candy thermometer.

Meanwhile, place the egg white in a large bowl.

Once the sugar mixture gets to around 255°F, start beating the egg white with an electric mixer on high until stiff peaks form. Slowly and carefully, stream the molten sugar into the egg white while beating continuously. Do not splash the molten sugar on the sides of the bowl because it hardens immediately.

Once all of the sugar is incorporated, continue to beat the mixture until it has the consistency of marshmallow fluff and holds its shape. It should take 3 to 4 minutes. Then, beat in the vanilla.

Working quickly, scoop the mixture into the prepared muffin cups. I use a cookie scoop that I spray with cooking spray between each scoop. Press a pecan half on top of each piece of candy.

If the day is very humid or if it's raining outside, the candy will take up to 12 hours to set. Leave it out, uncovered, at room temperature. If the day is dry, the candy should set in a few hours. It should have a texture similar to the circus peanut candy, and the wrapper should peel off easily from the candy. If not, let it sit at room temperature a few more hours.

MICROWAVE PEANUT BUTTER FUDGE

One more fudge recipe for you, this one is even easier than the last one. I love this plain, cut into squares, but I also love it on top of a pan of brownies for two. I call it a sugar bomb, and I love to be bombed.

Yield • about 8 pieces of fudge

¼ (60 grams) cup unsalted butter, diced

¼ cup (56 grams) regular creamy peanut butter

½ cup (28 grams) packed mini marshmallows

1 cup (100 grams) powdered sugar

LINE A 9 × 5 × 3-INCH LOAF PAN with parchment paper, leaving enough parchment overhang to form handles.

In a large glass bowl, combine the butter, peanut butter, and marshmallows. Cover the bowl with plastic wrap. Microwave on HIGH for 2 minutes.

Remove the plastic wrap, then stir in the powdered sugar all at once. Scrape the mixture into the prepared loaf pan, and let set in the fridge for 1 hour. Slice and serve.

»· PEPPERMINT PATTIES

When I get a craving for these minty little disks covered in dark chocolate, I know I can eat the whole bag. What's a girl to do? Make them herself at home, small batch style! This recipe makes a dozen peppermint patties. The damage is minimized, your sweet tooth is satisfied. Another small batch recipe for the win!

Yield • 12 patties

1 cup (100 grams) powdered sugar, plus more for dusting

2 teaspoon light corn syrup

2 teaspoon water

¼ teaspoon peppermint extract

4 ounces (113 grams) of dark chocolate

1 tablespoon solid vegetable shortening (or coconut oil)

PLACE THE POWDERED SUGAR in a medium-size bowl. Sprinkle with the water, corn syrup, and peppermint extract. Slowly stir the mixture. At first, it will seem as if the mixture won't come together, but stay with it. You can switch to an electric mixer on low speed, too. When it begins to clump, gather the mixture in your hands and knead it together. You should have a soft white dough that holds together well.

Take two 12-inch square pieces of parchment paper and dust with powdered sugar. Place the dough on one piece, dust with more powdered sugar, and cover with the other piece of parchment paper. Roll out the mixture to ¼-inch thickness. Keeping the dough between the two sheets of parchment paper, place it on a small baking sheet and freeze for 30 minutes.

Peel off the top layer of parchment and cut out as many circles as you can, using a 1 ½-inch cookie cutter. When you run out of space to cut, gather up the dough and roll it out again. You should get about twelve circles. Place the circles back on the parchment paper–lined cookie sheet and freeze solid for at least 1 hour.

When ready to dunk, melt the chocolate and shortening in a double boiler until smooth. Remove from the heat and let cool for a few minutes. Now, take the patties out of the freezer and dunk them *quickly* in the chocolate. Place them back on the sheet and freeze to set. Store in the freezer.

CHOCOLATE TRUFFLES...
with Bacon

What do you get the guy who has everything? These: a small box with six rich, dark chocolate truffles topped with a slow-cooked bacon bit. He'll never leave your side. Trust me.

Yield • 6 truffles

⅓ cup (80 mL) + 3 tablespoons (45 mL) heavy whipping cream, divided

4 ounces (113 grams) + 2 ounces (56 grams) chopped semisweet chocolate, divided

1 slice applewood smoked bacon

POUR THE ⅓ CUP OF CREAM into a deep, microwave-safe cup. Heat in the microwave on HIGH for 30 seconds, until small bubbles form around the edges. Remove from the microwave and add the 4 ounces of chocolate. Do not touch. Let sit for 1 minute.

Stir the chocolate mixture until smooth and melted. Pour into a shallow dish and place in the fridge until firm, about 30 minutes.

Meanwhile, place the bacon slice in a small skillet and cook over low heat, flipping often, until browned and cooked through, 10 to 15 minutes. Drain the slice on two paper towels. It will crisp as it cools. Crumble the bacon when cool.

Once the chocolate mixture is firm, scoop it into six small balls. Place on a plate, and freeze for 1 hour.

Melt the remaining 3 tablespoons of cream and 2 ounces of chocolate in the microwave, following the directions in step 1. Dunk the chilled chocolate truffles into this mixture. Place a piece of bacon on top of each truffle, and then return the truffles to the fridge to set.

Keep refrigerated until ready to serve.

Leftovers?

This business of scaling down desserts can leave you with quite a few leftover egg "parts." I tried to avoid it when possible, but a good portion of recipes in this book call for only egg whites or yolks. I highly recommend that you follow the instructions and not add an entire egg when only part of one is utilized in the recipe. I compiled a list of recipes to turn to when you have an extra egg white or yolk. Note: These recipes may or may not also call for an entire egg in addition to your leftover egg portion.

Recipes to use up an extra egg yolk

Recipes that use an extra egg white

Recipes that use up leftover sweetened condensed milk:

Acknowledgments

Because the process of writing a book is never a one-woman show…

I wish to acknowledge first and foremost, the dedication and hard work of my agent, Jean. She has believed in my 'for two' dreams from the beginning, and her support has never wavered. Thanks for steering me away from every skeevy opportunity, and putting me in touch with the most wonderful people to work with. You and I, lady—we're going to take on the world together.

And many thanks go to my team at Countryman Press. Without their support and belief, this book would not nearly be so pretty. Or, so typo-free. Thanks for being an absolute pleasure to work with, and for making me feel like a priority.

Index